ENTHUSIAST'S RESTORATION MANUAL

How to restore
Classic Largeframe Vespa Scooters

Rotary Valve 2-Strokes 1959 to 2008

YOUR illustrated guide to body and mechanical restoration

Mark Paxton

VELOCE PUBLISHING
THE PUBLISHER OF FINE AUTOMOTIVE BOOKS

Contents

Introduction........................6
  Why choose a rotary valve model?..6
  Using this book 6
  Models covered...............7
  Chassis numbers 8
  Engine numbers 8
  Parts........................8
  Project management.........9
  Tools........................9
  Workshop safety 9
  Disclaimer..................9
  Thanks......................9

Chapter 1. Power unit 10
  Engine removal............10
  Top end 14
  Flywheel and stator removal 17
  Clutch removal 19
  Rear brake removal 21
  Removing the carb 23
  Splitting the cases........24
  Crank removal/inspection 25
  Xmas tree removal 26
  Gearbox removal..........26
  Bearing removal from the cases 27
  Kickstart removal 27
  Case cleaning and inspection.....29
  Bearing replacement in cases.....30

  Crankshaft bearing refitting.........31
  Refitting crank 33
  Cush drive overhaul 33
  Gearbox strip and inspection......36
  Reassembly of cases 39
  Clutch overhaul 41
  Clutch refitting............46
  Rear hub reassembly 47
  Carb refitting 48
  Flywheel refitting 49
  Top end reassembly 49
  Selector box 51
  Engine mount replacement 52
  Refitting engine 54
  Starting up................56

Chapter 2. Fuel & exhaust 57
  Petrol tank removal/inspection ...57
  Fuel tap and line..........59
  Carburettor strip/overhaul..........61
  Exhaust system...........65

Chapter 3. Front end 66
  Headset strip early 66
  Headset strip PX 72
  Master cylinder...........75
  T5 Mark 1 headset 78
  Fork strip/overhaul (pre-PX) 78
  Fork strip/overhaul PX...........91

  Brake caliper 99
  Steering head bearings all.........102

Chapter 4. Frame 106
  Paint removal/assessment.........106
  Soda blasting 107
  Paint stripper............107
  Abrasives.................107
  Welding 108
  Dent removal 115
  Rust killing 115
  Side panels/mudguards/toolbox 117
  Brake pedal.............118
  Cables 119
  Steering locks 120

Chapter 5. Paint................123
  Decision time............123
  Colour choice............123
  Paint choice 123
  What you need to do it yourself.................124
  Preparation..............124
  Filler......................124
  Workshop and personal preparation 125
  New panels 125
  Masking off.............126

How to restore
Classic Largeframe Vespa Scooters

Rotary Valve 2-Strokes 1959 to 2008

Also from Veloce –

Speedpro Series
4-Cylinder Engine Short Block High-Performance Manual – New Updated & Revised Edition (Hammill)
Alfa Romeo DOHC High-performance Manual (Kartalamakis)
Alfa Romeo V6 Engine High-performance Manual (Kartalamakis)
BMC 998cc A-series Engine, How to Power Tune (Hammill)
1275cc A-series High-performance Manual (Hammill)
Camshafts – How to Choose & Time Them For Maximum Power (Hammill)
Competition Car Datalogging Manual, The (Templeman)
Cylinder Heads, How to Build, Modify & Power Tune – Updated & Revised Edition (Burgess & Gollan)
Distributor-type Ignition Systems, How to Build & Power Tune – New 3rd Edition (Hammill)
Fast Road Car, How to Plan and Build – Revised & Updated Colour New Edition (Stapleton)
Ford SOHC 'Pinto' & Sierra Cosworth DOHC Engines, How to Power Tune – Updated & Enlarged Edition (Hammill)
Ford V8, How to Power Tune Small Block Engines (Hammill)
Harley-Davidson Evolution Engines, How to Build & Power Tune (Hammill)
Holley Carburetors, How to Build & Power Tune – Revised & Updated Edition (Hammill)
Honda Civic Type R High-Performance Manual, The (Cowland & Clifford)
Jaguar XK Engines, How to Power Tune – Revised & Updated Colour Edition (Hammill)
Land Rover Discovery, Defender & Range Rover – How to Modify Coil Sprung Models for High Performance & Off-Road Action (Hosier)
MG Midget & Austin-Healey Sprite, How to Power Tune – Enlarged & updated 4th Edition (Hammill)
MGB 4-cylinder Engine, How to Power Tune (Burgess)
MGB V8 Power, How to Give Your – Third Colour Edition (Williams)
MGB, MGC & MGB V8, How to Improve – New 2nd Edition (Williams)
Mini Engines, How to Power Tune On a Small Budget – Colour Edition (Hammill)
Motorcycle-engined Racing Car, How to Build (Pashley)
Motorsport, Getting Started in (Collins)
Nissan GT-R High-performance Manual, The (Gorodji)
Nitrous Oxide High-performance Manual, The (Langfield)
Race & Trackday Driving Techniques (Hornsey)
Retro or classic car for high performance, How to modify your (Stapleton)
Rover V8 Engines, How to Power Tune (Hammill)
Secrets of Speed – Today's techniques for 4-stroke engine blueprinting & tuning (Swager)
Sportscar & Kitcar Suspension & Brakes, How to Build & Modify – Revised 3rd Edition (Hammill)
SU Carburettor High-performance Manual (Hammill)
Successful Low-Cost Rally Car, How to Build a (Young)
Suzuki 4x4, How to Modify For Serious Off-road Action (Richardson)
Tiger Avon Sportscar, How to Build Your Own – Updated & Revised 2nd Edition (Dudley)
TR2, 3 & TR4, How to Improve (Williams)
TR5, 250 & TR6, How to Improve (Williams)
TR7 & TR8, How to Improve (Williams)
V8 Engine, How to Build a Short Block For High Performance (Hammill)
Volkswagen Beetle Suspension, Brakes & Chassis, How to Modify For High Performance (Hale)
Volkswagen Bus Suspension, Brakes & Chassis for High Performance, How to Modify – Updated & Enlarged New Edition (Hale)
Weber DCOE, & Dellorto DHLA Carburetors, How to Build & Power Tune – 3rd Edition (Hammill)

RAC Handbooks
Caring for your bicycle – How to maintain & repair your bicycle (Henshaw)
Caring for your scooter – How to maintain & service your 49cc to 125cc twist & go scooter (Fry)
How your motorcycle works – Your guide to the components & systems of modern motorcycles (Henshaw)
Motorcycles – A first-time-buyer's guide (Henshaw)

Enthusiast's Restoration Manual Series
Beginner's Guide to Classic Motorcycle Restoration, The (Burns)
Citroën 2CV, How to Restore (Porter)
Classic Large Frame Vespa Scooters, How to Restore (Paxton)
Classic Car Bodywork, How to Restore (Thaddeus)
Classic British Car Electrical Systems (Astley)
Classic Car Electrics (Thaddeus)
Classic Cars, How to Paint (Thaddeus)
Ducati Bevel Twins 1971 to 1986 (Falloon)
How to Restore Classic Off-road Motorcycles (Burns)
How to restore Honda CX500 & CX650 – YOUR step-by-step colour illustrated guide to complete restoration (Burns)
How to restore Honda Fours – YOUR step-by-step colour illustrated guide to complete restoration (Burns)
Jaguar E-type (Crespin)
Reliant Regal, How to Restore (Payne)
Triumph TR2, 3, 3A, 4 & 4A, How to Restore (Williams)
Triumph TR5/250 & 6, How to Restore (Williams)
Triumph TR7/8, How to Restore (Williams)
Triumph Trident T150/T160 & BSA Rocket III, How to Restore (Rooke)
Ultimate Mini Restoration Manual, The (Ayre & Webber)
Volkswagen Beetle, How to Restore (Tyler)
VW Bay Window Bus (Paxton)
Yamaha FS1-E, How to Restore (Watts)

Expert Guides
Land Rover Series I-III – Your expert guide to common problems & how to fix them (Thurman)
MG Midget & A-H Sprite – Your expert guide to common problems & how to fix them (Horler)

Essential Buyer's Guide Series
BMW Boxer Twins – All air-cooled R45, R50, R60, R65, R75, R80, R90, R100, RS, RT & LS (Not GS) models 1969 to 1994 (Henshaw)
BSA 350 & 500 Unit Construction Singles (Henshaw)
BSA 500 & 650 Twins (Henshaw)
BSA Bantam (Henshaw)
Citroën 2CV (Paxton)
Choosing, Using & Maintaining Your Electric Bicycle (Henshaw)
Ducati Bevel Twins (Falloon)
Ducati Desmodue Twins (Falloon)
Ducati Desmoquattro Twins – 851, 888, 916, 996, 998, ST4 1988 to 2004 (Falloon)
Ford Capri (Paxton)
Harley-Davidson Big Twins (Henshaw)
Hinckley Triumph triples & fours 750, 900, 955, 1000, 1050, 1200 – 1991-2009 (Henshaw)
Honda CBR FireBlade (Henshaw)
Honda CBR600 Hurricane (Henshaw)
Honda SOHC Fours 1969-1984 (Henshaw)
Kawasaki Z1 & Z900 (Orritt)
Land Rover Series I, II & IIA (Thurman)
Mini (Paxton)
Moto Guzzi 2-valve big twins (Falloon)
Norton Commando (Henshaw)
Piaggio Scooters – all modern four-stroke automatic models 1991 to 2016 (Willis)
Royal Enfield Bullet (Henshaw)
Triumph 350 & 500 Twins (Henshaw)
Triumph Bonneville (Henshaw)
Triumph Thunderbird, Trophy & Tiger (Henshaw)
Velocette 350 & 500 Singles (Henshaw)
Vespa Scooters – Classic 2-stroke models 1960-2008 (Paxton)

General
Automotive A-Z, Lane's Dictionary of Automotive Terms (Lane)

Bonjour – Is this Italy? (Turner)
British 250cc Racing Motorcycles (Pereira)
British Café Racers (Cloesen)
British Custom Motorcycles – The Brit Chop – choppers, cruisers, bobbers & trikes (Cloesen)
BSA Bantam Bible, The (Henshaw)
BSA Motorcycles – the final evolution (Jones)
Ducati 750 Bible, The (Falloon)
Ducati 750 SS 'round-case' 1974, The Book of the (Falloon)
Ducati 860, 900 and Mille Bible, The (Falloon)
Ducati Monster Bible (New Updated & Revised Edition), The (Falloon)
Ducati 916 (updated edition) (Falloon)
Fine Art of the Motorcycle Engine, The (Peirce)
From Crystal Palace to Red Square – A Hapless Biker's Road to Russia (Turner)
Funky Mopeds (Skelton)
Italian Cafe Racers (Cloesen)
Italian Custom Motorcycles (Cloesen)
Japanese Custom Motorcycles – The Nippon Chop – Chopper, Cruiser, Bobber, Trikes and Quads (Cloesen)
Kawasaki Triples Bible, The (Walker)
Kawasaki Z1 Story, The (Sheehan)
Lambretta Bible, The (Davies)
Laverda Twins & Triples Bible 1968-1986 (Falloon)
Lea-Francis Story, The (Price)
Little book of trikes, the (Quellin)
Moto Guzzi Sport & Le Mans Bible, The (Falloon)
Motorcycle Apprentice (Cakebread)
Motorcycle GP Racing in the 1960s (Pereira)
Motorcycle Road & Racing Chassis Designs (Noakes)
MV Agusta Fours, The book of the classic (Falloon)
The Norton Commando Bible – All models 1968 to 1978 (Henshaw)
Peking to Paris 2007 (Young)
Racing Line – British motorcycle racing in the golden age of the big single (Guntrip)
Roads with a View – England's greatest views and how to find them by road (Corfield)
Scooters & Microcars, The A-Z of Popular (Dan)
Scooter Lifestyle (Grainger)
SCOOTER MANIA! – Recollections of the Isle of Man International Scooter Rally (Jackson)
Triumph Bonneville Bible (59-83) (Henshaw)
Triumph Bonneville!, Save the – The inside story of the Meriden Workers' Co-op (Rosamond)
Triumph Motorcycles & the Meriden Factory (Hancox)
Triumph Speed Twin & Thunderbird Bible (Woolridge)
Triumph Tiger Cub Bible (Estall)
Triumph Trophy Bible (Woolridge)
Triumph TR6 (Kimberley)
TT Talking – The TT's most exciting era – As seen by Manx Radio TT's lead commentator 2004-2012 (Lambert)
Velocette Motorcycles – MSS to Thruxton – New Third Edition (Burris)
Vespa – The Story of a Cult Classic in Pictures (Uhlig)
Vincent Motorcycles: The Untold Story since 1946 (Guyony & Parker)

Veloce Publishing's other imprints:

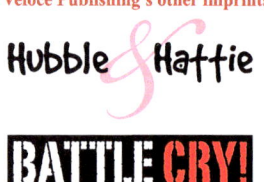

For post publication news, updates and amendments relating to this book please scan the QR code or visit www.veloce.co.uk/books/V5028

www.veloce.co.uk

First published in May 2012 by Veloce Publishing Limited, Veloce House, Parkway Farm Business Park, Middle Farm Way, Poundbury, Dorchester, Dorset, DT1 3AR, England. Fax 01305 250479/e-mail info@veloce.co.uk/web www.veloce.co.uk or www.velocebooks.com. Reprinted September 2016.

ISBN: 978-1-787110-28-1 UPC: 6-36847-01028-7

© Mark Paxton and Veloce Publishing 2012 and 2016. All rights reserved. With the exception of quoting brief passages for the purpose of review, no part of this publication may be recorded, reproduced or transmitted by any means, including photocopying, without the written permission of Veloce Publishing Ltd. Throughout this book logos, model names and designations, etc, have been used for the purposes of identification, illustration and decoration. Such names are the property of the trademark holder as this is not an official publication.
Readers with ideas for automotive books, or books on other transport or related hobby subjects, are invited to write to the editorial director of Veloce Publishing at the above address.
British Library Cataloguing in Publication Data – A catalogue record for this book is available from the British Library.
Typesetting, design and page make-up all by Veloce Publishing Ltd on Apple Mac. Printed and bound by CPI Group (UK) Ltd, Croydon, CR0 4YY.

CONTENTS

Etch (again) 126
Primer......................................126
Sealer 127
Primer again 127
Top coats................................127
Finishing touches 127
Small parts 128
Painting plastic.......................128

Chapter 6. Electrics...................129
Wiring loom 129
Headlight.................................131
Tail-light 131
Indicators 131
Switchgear/instruments
  /brakelight switch..................132
Horn 133

Ignition....................................133
Charging system 136
Starter motor 137
Converting to 12-volt 137

Chapter 7. Trim 138
Badges/panel trim...................138
Floor runners 140
Seats 142
Speedometers........................144
Stands 145
Horncast..................................146
Legshield trim........................146
Rubber parts 148
Toolbox locks 148
Spare wheel covers................149
Helmet locks 149

Chapter 8. Wheels 150
Rims 150
Tyre replacement....................150
Stud replacement...................151

Chapter 9. Maintenance............153
Weekly check 153
Every 1500 miles/2500km........153
Every 3000 miles/5000km.......153
Every 6000 miles/10,000km......153
Every 12000 miles/20,000km....153
Every 24000/40,000km 153
Fuel and oil.............................153
Cables....................................154
Storage...................................154

Index 159

Introduction

The Vespa scooter is one of only a handful of mass-produced vehicles that have transcended their original design brief – in this case providing cheap transport for the masses – to become not only an immediately recognisable symbol of their country of origin, but also a universally-hailed design icon. The secret of the Vespa's success was combining style with unrivalled practicality, finished off with a level of reliability virtually unmatched by other two wheelers of the era, regardless of cost. The design evolved subtly but significantly over the years, ensuring that its virtues remained relevant to its loyal buyers; so much so that despite going out of production in 2008, Piaggio subsequently decided that the legend must not be allowed to die, and, as this book was being put together, the first of the resurrected PXs was rolling down the lines at Pontedera once more.

WHY CHOOSE A ROTARY VALVE MODEL?

The scooters of the post-1959 era provide the very best of the Vespa experience. They are easy to find, cheap to buy, straightforward to restore and simple to maintain. This combination provides the perfect classic ride without any major drawbacks, such as having to track down rare and expensive parts. As a manufacturer Piaggio clearly believed in the evolution of the range, ensuring that any major problems were ironed out over time, and making these scooters among the most dependable machines of their time. More importantly perhaps, they are also tremendously engaging to own and enjoy.

USING THIS BOOK

This volume makes no pretence at being a comprehensive workshop guide for every variant of largeframe, rotary valve Vespa made. Instead it seeks to cover major tasks in some detail, and should be used in conjunction with a traditional manual and perhaps more importantly, a copy of the original parts book for your particular model. Scans of these parts

Before starting a restoration, gather as much information about your scooter as possible – it will be invaluable as the restoration progresses.

books are freely available online with most rotary valve variants covered, so download and print off a copy.

This is a guide to renovation, restoration and repair, some of which includes the use of non-standard parts. If you intend a complete rebuild to the original factory specifications, it would be wise to invest in the relevant volume in the *Vespa Tecnica* series. Books 2, 3 and 5 cover the rotary valve period and show the scooters in their original state. They are expensive, and if you decide you

INTRODUCTION

Dented, rusty, and almost completely worn out mechanically, this Motovespa Sprint was an ideal restoration candidate.

It ended up looking a little different by the end – fully refurbished and fitted with a later rotary valve engine to replace the piston-ported original. The techniques used are all described within the pages of this book.

as another sizeable volume would be needed to cover the topic in any detail. However, suggestions for a few basic updates have been included, which could make the day-to-day use of your old Vespa more pleasurable. It is probably best to read the book through completely to get a feel for the whole process before diving into your particular restoration. On occasion the picture sequence may show parts, fitted or missing, that may not have been covered in the text to that point. This is because there are many ways to rebuild an engine, for example, so it is best to stick with the procedure laid out in the text until you have developed your own preferences.

MODELS COVERED

The scooters built in the period covered by this book fall into three main categories: the VBB type, built at the beginning of the run until the early to mid-1960s; its successor, the Sprint type, which has slightly more angular lines; and last but certainly not least, with over 2.5 million produced, the P series, which continues to be made today. These rough categories will therefore be used throughout the book to save the repetitive listing of models individually.

VBB type
Includes 150/VBA/VBB/GL.

Pros
These scooters have more voluptuous styling than their successors and therefore have a more recognisably classic outline. They are very reliable in standard form.

Cons
Their 8in wheels give a twitchy ride, limit brake efficiency as the drums are obviously smaller and restrict tyre choice. Reliability is assured through a low power output, but this makes their use on major roads a daunting

need volume 6 with its additional paint swatches, be prepared for a wallet-busting experience.

All the work contained in these pages has been done by the author, as there really is no substitute for personal experience in order to get a feel for the effort, skill or nerve-jangling frustration involved in the restoration process. The techniques outlined may differ from those advocated by some, but they all work, as several rusty, non-running scooters were successfully resurrected whilst creating this book. Tuning has mainly been ignored,

HOW TO RESTORE CLASSIC LARGEFRAME VESPA SCOOTERS

The VBB type can be easily recognised by its 8in wheels, bulbous side panels, and wide legshields.

prospect. They suffer from bouncy front suspension.

Sprint type
Includes Super/Sprint/GT/Rally/Sprint Veloce/GTR/TS.

Pros
10in wheels on all models except the Super, so better braking and tyres. More power than previous models but still reliable, the extra grunt coming at the expense of slightly higher fuel consumption. Still stylish looking scooters, and useable on today's roads.

Cons
6-volt electrics. The front suspension is still soft with some of the braking improvements being transferred into fork dive rather than retardation.

P series
Includes P125 and 150X/P200E/PX80, 125, 150, 200/T5.

Pros
Better brakes, suspension, roadholding and engine than the preceding models, with the added benefit of 12-volt electrics.

Cons
Rather bland, squared-off styling.

There is a degree of overlap between each of these types (and even the models within them at times) and 'crossover' scooters are not uncommon, especially when model

The Rally is generally regarded as the ultimate expression of the Sprint type. The styling of this series was more angular than the VBB, and generally slimmed down for a sleeker look.

The P range was intended to be the penultimate stage in the evolution of Piaggio's metal-bodied geared scooter, as the Cosa that came later was meant to replace it. The styling was squared off, and indicators were standard apart from a very short run at the beginning of production. More than 2.5 million have been produced, and the Pontedera factory has begun knocking them out again from mid-2011. The P series soldiers on.

variants supplied to different markets are taken into account.

CHASSIS NUMBERS
Up until the end of Sprint production the chassis number was generally stamped into the frame under the left-hand panel towards the rear. UK-built scooters of that era had a riveted alloy plate on the right side, sometimes replacing proper frame stamping. On the Rally and P series scooters the number is under the right-hand side panel near the locating pin hole at the back of the engine. In addition, some scooters had alloy plates attached to the central tunnel or to the frame near the petrol tap lever, depending on the market for which they were destined.

ENGINE NUMBERS
The engine code and number are stamped into the left-hand side crankcase half in the swinging arm, visible behind the exhaust downpipe. The code is particularly useful when ordering spares.

PARTS
This is rather a vexing subject, but one that needs mentioning before you plough on with your restoration, as it may influence some of your decisions. Many of the new bits bought for the scooters restored within these pages were of poor quality, and far inferior to the original parts that had been removed. It is probably safer to re-use as much of the original scooter as you can, although it will probably mean a longer and more expensive rebuild. The best option when you do have to buy new bits is to use genuine Piaggio spares, and if they are not available then something manufactured in Europe (although the floor pans fitted during these restorations all came from Vietnam and were superb – there will always be exceptions). Several well-known suppliers in the UK were used, both as a mail order client and

INTRODUCTION

as a personal caller. One of the large German suppliers that advertises in the UK magazines was also tried out. The service received from all of them was very good, but there really is no substitute for using a local shop as they can (and in my case did) warn about poor quality bits, or at the very least provide the information to make an informed choice as to where a few pennies might be saved. Having the part in your hand to examine before paying out your hard earned cash is a big advantage, so use your local shop – it might be slightly more expensive than an online auction house, for example, but it only takes the purchase of one useless bit to wipe out any savings you may have made up to that point.

PROJECT MANAGEMENT

A rather grand concept, but planning your restoration makes a lot of sense. The whole project will be a juggling act between the conflicting forces of time, money and ability, with their eventual proportions differing with each individual restorer. All the skills needed to renovate your Vespa can be learnt by most people, but if you need it all doing quickly then you are going to have to hand over bits of the build to professionals rather than go through a potentially long and tricky learning curve to hone your abilities.

Vespas can easily be broken down into large sub-assemblies which can then be dealt with individually. Use a digital camera to record the process as it will jog your memory later as you struggle to remember where a cable ran or if a washer had been fitted. A note pad is a good idea as well, to list parts which need replacing.

A possible plan of action could be:
- Remove side panels and seat followed by:
  – Petrol tank
  – Engine unit
  – Headset
  – Front forks
- Strip the rest of the frame, cables, stand, trim, pedals etc
- Frame blasting/repairs
- Paint

If you are going to let someone else handle the body repairs or paint for example, you can proceed with overhauling the forks or engine whilst the work is being done elsewhere. The decision as to which sub-assembly to do first is very much a personal choice. Reassembly involves simply reversing the strip procedure, bolting your restored bits back on to the newly-painted frame.

TOOLS

There are only a few dedicated special tools that are required during the restoration, and these are mentioned in the text. They are all relatively inexpensive and even if you only intend doing one scooter they can always be sold on again afterwards. Frame repairs will mean access to a welder and for paint application a compressor and gun. Even DIY models are a considerable investment, but will save money in the long-term. Hand tools should be of decent quality – not many are needed, so buy the best you can afford. It's much better to fork out on a good ratchet and a handful of quality sockets than on a giant set filled with sizes you will never use, and which will quickly break after rounding off any tight fittings you might come across.

WORKSHOP SAFETY

Restoring any vehicle, even a relatively small one like a Vespa scooter, will throw up potentially dangerous situations during the process. Do not rush, take time to assess the task in hand, and visualise any potential hazards that may result. Read any literature supplied with power tools before use. Mains electricity is a killer, so a circuit breaker is essential. Fuel should be drained before work begins, and stored in sealed containers designed for the purpose. At least one fire extinguisher should be on hand at all times. Welding and grinding can send sparks over a considerable distance, so make sure there are no flammable materials in range. Always leave half an hour spare at the end of each session working on the scooter to clear up and put the tools away – this will give time for anything that might be quietly smouldering to show up before you call it a day. Protect your eyes and lungs from dust and fumes, and be aware that old brake linings could contain asbestos. Wear appropriate clothing for the task in hand – thick cotton is the best material for overalls, and wear stout boots. Use a barrier cream on your hands before starting, and a dedicated hand cleaner with a moisturising agent afterwards. Remember to protect the environment as well, disposing of old oil, waste metal, plastics etc at your local recycling site.

DISCLAIMER

The author, publisher and retailer cannot accept any liability for personal injury, financial loss or mechanical damage endured as a result of any information included or omitted from this volume.

THANKS

At times in any restoration a helping hand is required to deal with a stubborn fixing, or to provide a second opinion as to whether the final body preparation is really up to scratch. My thanks must go to my mate, Tony, once again for his assistance throughout the process.

Chapter 1
Power unit

ENGINE REMOVAL

The power units of all the rotary valve models are very similar in design and construction. The frame mount remained the same throughout production, so the motors are interchangeable, although some modifications to wiring, exhausts, rear shock mounting bolt and centre stands may be required. Removing the engine unit is straightforward and relatively quick, so much so that even in the case of some simple repairs it is easier to get the unit out of the frame and on to a workbench for any rectification work.

01.1 All the largeframe engines sit behind a removable cowl on the right-hand side of the scooter.

01.2 The carb box lid is secured with two screws at the outer edge (arrowed) – undo them and lift the lid away. The air filter is then removed by undoing the two screws each side of the taller throttle stop screw.

POWER UNIT

01.3 The choke and throttle cable ends revealed. If you push the choke lever with a screwdriver, the loop of the cable can be wiggled free. The same technique will release the throttle cable, although fighting against the slide return spring makes it slightly trickier. If the scooter has autolube, the cable is attached to the pump with the carb slide operated by a bent rod sitting in an adjacent hole in the lever.

01.4 To get the petrol pipe off, ignore the securing clip and undo the banjo union bolt, but make sure the petrol tank tap is turned off first. There will be some spillage of fuel, more if the tap is not working correctly, so be prepared to clamp the pipe if necessary until you have something to drain the fuel into. The banjo can then be pulled out of the pipe, which can be pushed down and out of the carb box.

01.5 The oil feed pipe needs to have this clip undone and the flexible pipe pulled free. Have a suitably sized bolt to plug the end of the pipe, to prevent oil leaking out.

01.6 Open the wiring junction box, split the connector or undo the post securing screws (depending on model), then lift the rubber boot over the coil and disconnect the wires.

01.7 Drain the gearbox oil. The plug is helpfully marked 'olio' to avoid mistakes.

01.8 Remove the two nuts and washers holding the selector box to the crankcase. More oil will be released, so place a container underneath. Disconnect the cables from the box.

HOW TO RESTORE CLASSIC LARGEFRAME VESPA SCOOTERS

01.9 Under the engine, release the brake cable securing nut and the screwed nipple that secures the clutch cable, and pull both away from the motor and free of the adjusting sleeves cast into the swinging arm. The brake cable can be awkward, as it is thick and often badly distorted from being clamped. If the cables are to be renewed anyway, it may be simpler just to cut them.

01.10 The exhaust can now come off. It's perfectly possible to get the engine out with it still attached, but it often sticks to the cylinder stub, and is easier to get free whilst the motor is still securely attached to the frame. There is a mounting bolt (17mm head) in front of the wheel and into the swinging arm, which is also often stuck – apply lots of releasing oil and keep turning it to persuade it to free. The wheel needs to be removed to get it out.

01.11 To get the back wheel off support the rear of the frame, in this case with a block of wood and a scissor jack.

01.12 The downpipe mount is a clamp held by a 13mm nut. T5 engines (and some LML) differ in the downpipe mounting, which in their case is a flange bolted to two studs on the barrel. These fittings are often corroded, so douse them well with penetrating fluid before trying to get them off.

01.13 With the clamp loosened, use a soft drift (a wooden shaft in this case) and tap down to free the exhaust.

01.14 The main pivot nut needs to be undone. It might take some persuading if it hasn't moved for some time.

POWER UNIT

01.15 With the nut off, tap out the main pivot bolt through the frame

01.16 Once it is out a short way, support the cylinder, then pull it completely free.

01.17 There is enough movement in the rear shock to allow the engine to be twisted and turned slightly away from the frame. The mounting bolt can be undone; support the back of the engine and pull it free from the shock absorber and its mount. The power unit is now ready to be transferred to the workbench for stripping.

01.18 If you prefer, the exhaust and wheel can be left in place until later, in which case the unit can be wheeled out once the mounting pin and shock bolt have been removed.

01.19 If the pivot bolt is seized in the metal sleeves of the mountings, which is far from rare, turn the scooter over. This will probably reveal a cruddy mess like this. On the side with the bolt head you can clearly see the gap between motor and frame.

01.20 Using a slim plasma cutting disc on an angle grinder, cut through the bolt shaft. There is usually enough wiggle room to get the motor out without a second cut on the other side.

HOW TO RESTORE CLASSIC LARGEFRAME VESPA SCOOTERS

TOP END
Cylinder head removal/inspection

The cylinder head is made from light alloy, and should be checked for fin damage or signs of cracking around the stud holes and the sparkplug thread. De-coking should be carried out with a non-metallic scraper – an old toothbrush handle cut at a 45 degree angle is a good starting point. The head should be checked for warping, which can be easily done by taping some fine grade wet-and-dry paper to a known flat surface, eg a sheet of glass, then lubricating it with light oil and moving the mating surface of the head over it in a series of random circular motions for a minute or two. When you are finished the alloy should be an even light silver across the whole of the sealing ring. If there are patches where it remains discoloured, the head is not flat. Alternatively, spray some black paint on the head joint before rubbing with a sanding block to make any imperfections even more easily visible. Fortunately, new heads are available for most models, and are cheap.

01.21 The cylinder head cowl – metal on early engines, plastic later – is held on by a bolt on top ...

01.22 ... plus two screws at the side. This is the lower one.

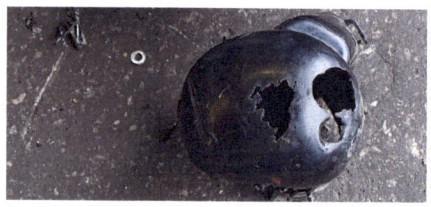

01.23 The cowl then pulls off, revealing the cylinder head. Check the cowl for damage: it must be complete and free from cracks if it is to do its job properly. This one is obviously scrap.

01.24 The cylinder head securing nuts are 11mm for 125/150cc engines and 13mm for 200cc. The nuts should be undone by one turn each in a diagonal sequence to release pressure on the head, before completely undoing them for removal.

01.25 Don't worry if the cylinder stud comes out instead of the nut undoing. It can be easily resolved later.

01.26 The cylinder head is now free and can be removed. Check the smooth circular ring that sits against the barrel for signs of escaped gases – it will show up as a stain with possible pockmarks in the alloy. Carbon build-up in the combustion chamber is inevitable.

01.27 Left: The old carbon should be scraped off with a non-metallic implement, such as this old toothbrush, which has had the handle cut off at a 45 degree angle to give it an edge.
01.28 Right: With most of the carbon removed, wipe away any remaining soft deposits, then use fine wet-and-dry paper lubricated with a little penetrating oil, and work the surface to a shine. This will discourage any future build-up when the engine is put back into service.

POWER UNIT

Piston and barrel – inspection for wear

Pistons should be checked for blow-by, gouging or scoring, and damage to the crown. Replacements are easily found for later models, but over-sizes for VBB era scooters are harder to track down. Barrels should be examined for scoring, signs of a wear lip near the top of the bore, alloy debris from a seized piston, and fin damage. Standard replacement barrels with pistons offer an economic way out of trouble and can be found in two port layout (virtually everything pre PX) and three port for the later engines.

Disc-braked PXs have matched pistons and barrels, a code letter is stamped on each, so if replacing one only then make sure to match the letter.

01.30 As you pull the barrel, support the piston to stop it dropping onto the studs and also to catch any debris such as broken piston rings. This is actually a Malossi kit, which has larger than standard piston ports.

01.29 With the head removed the barrel can be pulled free. As it is cast iron (not T5) expect it to be rusty. It can be blasted and painted with heat-resistant paint if it is to be re-used and you can't live with the rust.

01.31 The cylinder can often be stuck on the studs, resisting all attempts to pull it free. If that is the case, lock two of the head nuts on each stud in turn. Then unscrew the bottom one, which will turn the stud and free it from the barrel and case at the same time. Once all four are out, the barrel should come off easily. If the piston is seized in the barrel leave it for the moment – it can come off when the crank is released as long as the studs are out.

01.33 The piston is held to the conrod by a pin, which is secured on each side by circlips like this.

01.32 Check the barrel for scoring. If any is visible, run a fingernail over it – if the nail catches where it's marked, it will need reboring. There may be a carbon ring around the very top edge of the barrel, which isn't a problem, it can be removed, but check about 25mm down from the top at 90 degrees from the gudgeon pin, feeling for a lip where the rings have been running. Once again, if you can feel it with your fingertips a rebore is required. If there is any doubt, your local scooter shop or engine reconditioners will be happy to give an opinion.

HOW TO RESTORE CLASSIC LARGEFRAME VESPA SCOOTERS

01.34 The clips have very small eye holes and require dedicated pliers to remove them.

01.35 Just remove one for the time being, then warm the piston around the gudgeon pin with a hot air gun. The pin can then be pushed though using a flat-bladed screwdriver or similar. They are often a tight fit – if that is the case, refit the barrel to support the piston then gently tap out the pin. If you do not support the piston you stand a real risk of bending the conrod.

be serviceable. If that is the case there should be an identifying letter stamped in the bore and on the piston, like the PX models mentioned previously. Genuine piston rings are expensive for these models, but cheap ones may cause damage to the Nicasil, so fitting non-genuine parts is very much a false economy.

Gudgeon pin/little end

Pins can be stiff, so a little heat may be needed to remove them. There is a dedicated tool for the job, but it isn't necessary as long as you support the piston during pin removal if you choose to tap it out. Wear can be spotted in the form of ridging where the little end bearing has run. The bearing itself is harder to check as the rollers usually just get looser in their cage, but this bearing should be an automatic replacement anyway. Disc models have colour-coded little end bearings matching a dab of paint on the conrod, or notches cut in the rod.

T5

Unlike all the other rotary valve models the T5 has an aluminium barrel with a Nicasil lining, which means reboring is not an option. It is possible to have the barrel recoated, assuming there are no deep gouges, but replacement is usually the best solution to wear. Neither choice is cheap. The main wear checks are the same as with an iron barrel, but in addition look for signs of flaking in the coating.

It is perfectly possible with a coated bore that the piston can be worn yet the barrel still

01.36 The little end bearing is released by removing the pin. Check it for scuff marks or sloppy rollers, or even better, replace it as a matter of course every time the top end is stripped.

01.37 The pin itself should be checked for grooves or heat discolouration where the little end bearing runs.

01.38 Pistons should not show a lot of discolouration below the rings – this blow-by is a sure sign of ring or bore wear. The sides of the piston may be scored: if so, use the fingernail test once more or, if budget allows, just replace.

POWER UNIT

FLYWHEEL AND STATOR REMOVAL

The flywheel will usually require a special tool to remove it. Some models have a self-extracting version where the centre nut backs out against a circlip, which then forces off the flywheel. Often this circlip is missing, a replacement will have to be found and fitted before removal is possible. Don't be tempted to use a leg type puller, as the light alloy fan will crack long before the taper releases its grip. Once the flywheel is off its taper it may still feel reluctant to come away, this is only due to the pull of the magnets.

01.39 To gain access to the flywheel the cover must be unscrewed.

01.40 There will be a cover in the middle that needs to be prised out, although it is often missing. Under the cover will be the flywheel securing nut (19mm head).

01.41 The flywheel can be locked to aid removal of the securing nut by either passing a socket extension bar through the conrod eye and pulling it down on to the cases, which should be protected with thick card or pieces of wood, or by using a dedicated holder as pictured here. It needs the small tag (arrowed) bending out slightly to make it sit more securely against the fins. The cowling screws are used to hold it in position.

01.42 With the flywheel secured, remove the nut and the wavy washer underneath.

01.43 To get the flywheel off you will need a puller. It just screws in, but make sure that it is fully down or the threads may strip when pressure is applied. The central bolt is then screwed in, which pulls the flywheel off. It is often very slow to relinquish its grip.

HOW TO RESTORE CLASSIC LARGEFRAME VESPA SCOOTERS

01.44 The stator plate lies underneath. This is an electronic version, the points setup is similar in layout, and is covered more fully in the ignition section.

01.45 Make sure the timing marks are clear and lined up.

01.46 If they're not or you're unsure, add some of your own, making certain that the scratches are deep enough to withstand any cleaning that the cases may be subjected to later.

01.47 The screws are tight, or should be. The screwdriver must fit the heads snugly or they will round off.

01.48 The stator wiring will pull down the hole in the casting if the junction box is removed first. It simply levers out of the case.

01.49 The stator plate pulls free of the casing, and the wiring can be pulled gently down through the cast tube (arrowed) and away from the motor.

POWER UNIT

01.50 Pre-P series motors look slightly different, with a larger casting around the crank that is clearly visible with the stator out of the way.

01.51 Remove the woodruff key and put it somewhere safe. Make sure the crankshaft slot is undamaged.

01.51a The woodruff key itself should also be checked for wear to the sides, which should be smooth and ridge-free. Replacements are cheap.

01.52 The oil seal can be carefully prised from the case and discarded (P series).

CLUTCH REMOVAL

01.53 The clutch covers all look pretty much the same. They are held on by three 8mm bolts on late engines, and 10mm on the earlier versions. The cover can be eased off by gently pulling the attached lever backward and forward.

01.54 Clutches prior to the Cosa version (which was fitted late EFL, approximately 1995 on) look like this. The Cosa version has a smooth face without the cups.

01.55 There is a wire clip passing through two holes in a release plate on all types. Insert a screwdriver blade under the wire at the larger hole and push down – the cover will come free.

19

HOW TO RESTORE CLASSIC LARGEFRAME VESPA SCOOTERS

01.56 Underneath is the clutch retaining nut. There is a locking washer with one tab bent into the nut slots. Bend it back out of the way. Cosa versions have a locking nut instead: see later.

01.57 You will now need this special clutch nut removing tool to get the nut undone.

01.58 A clutch holding tool is useful, although you could also lock the conrod to hold the crankshaft whilst the clutch nut is undone.

01.59 One end sits over one of the cover-retaining bolts, which is screwed back into the case. The other end pushes into the basket between the plates.

01.60 Once locked, the centre nut can be undone.

01.61 The clutch nut can be removed, followed by the locking washer. This washer should be replaced each time the clutch is removed.

01.62 The Cosa clutch fitted to disc braked PX models does without the locking washer and castellated nut, having what looks like a normal nut instead.

POWER UNIT

01.63 If you look closely, the nut appears misshapen. This is correct, as the ovality acts as a self-locking mechanism. It is also possible that a normal nut (M12) and wavy washer was fitted at the factory.

01.64 The whole assembly (both types) can then be pulled from the crank. It may be stuck – if so, use two screwdrivers as levers and gently pry it off.

01.65 Behind the clutch there is a spacer, either plain like this ...

01.66 ... or toothed and part of the autolube drive like this (arrowed). Either way, it just slides off.

01.67 Remove the woodruff key and store somewhere safe.

REAR BRAKE REMOVAL

01.68 Remove the split pin and locking cover, and undo the nut.

HOW TO RESTORE CLASSIC LARGEFRAME VESPA SCOOTERS

01.69 With the drum off the shoes are exposed, as is the rear hub oil seal assembly, which in this case is leaking (arrowed) – a very common occurence.

01.70 Remove these little horseshoe clips by spreading the open ends with your fingers. Be careful, as they tend to suddenly spring free.

01.71 Turn the operating lever to slightly lift the shoes from the cam. Open them more with a screwdriver, whilst lifting the other end of the shoe from the static pin until one shoe is free, which will release the tension on the return spring, allowing both to be lifted from the backplate.

01.72 If the shoes are contaminated don't try cleaning them, no matter how little wear they have; renew them.

01.73 The backplate is held by three self-tapping screws ...

01.74 ... once they are removed the plate can be lifted clear. There are rubber sealing rings around the main casting, the shoe pivots, and the operating cam casting. Remove and discard; replacements are very cheap.

22

POWER UNIT

01.75 On late EFL PX a metal dust cover is visible, as the oil seal found on other models was moved inside. Carefully lever out the cover, as it can be re-used if undamaged. If a rubber seal is fitted here, it too can be prised out.

01.76 Under the dust cover there is a sealed bearing. The output shaft oil seal is underneath the bearing, as already stated, and although this setup offers better resistance to leaks and subsequent shoe contamination, it means an engine strip when the seal does eventually go. If a rubber seal was fitted here then the bearing will not be a sealed type, but instead open and lubricated by the gearbox oil.

01.77 Early rotaries have a castellated securing ring holding the seal in place.

01.78 Remove this securing clip, then undo the ring which has a reverse thread, so turns clockwise to undo. A special tool should be used but the ring can normally be turned using a carefully applied drift.

REMOVING THE CARB

When removing either type of carb fitting, ensure that loose washers don't fall into the engine if a full strip is not on the cards. Turn the crank to close the inlet port before removing the securing bolts or nuts.

01.79 The carburettor is held in place by two sleeved bolts on most versions up to late EFL PX.

HOW TO RESTORE CLASSIC LARGEFRAME VESPA SCOOTERS

01.80 Late carbs have socket headed securing bolts like this. Take care removing these bolts regardless of type as there are loose washers under both which could fall into the motor. The flat washer is a special size so keep them with the bolts.

01.81 Pulling the carb free from its box may be difficult on late motors, as the idle adjustment is from this protruding bolt head, which passes through a tight-fitting seal. If there are problems, just push the seal into the box with a small screwdriver then wiggle the carb out.

01.82 The carb box is secured by this single screw (arrowed) which may be obscured by the gasket. Undo and remove the carb box, complete with autolube pump (where fitted).

SPLITTING THE CASES

The engine internals are held in the left-hand crankcase, so splitting the cases essentially means lifting away the right-hand side. The engine studs have D-shaped heads that hold them in place and prevent them turning whilst their nuts are loose. If the cases are reluctant to split do not lever them with a screwdriver, gently tap them with a soft-faced hammer. If things remain stuck then there is probably still a case bolt in place so check again. On pre-PX models the cases can be reluctant to part, so the right-hand side will need to have heat applied around the main bearing area to encourage movement.

01.83 Undo the case bolts and remove them completely. It is probably a good idea to lay them out in sequence to make replacement easier later on.

01.84 There are four nuts inside the stator recess. Undo them diagonally to release pressure before removing completely.

01.85 The cases should open fairly easily, if they don't there is probably a fitting that has been forgotten. Go back and double-check.

01.86 The cases may stick before they are fully parted. If so, move the kickstart lever down and they should release. A gentle tap from a soft-faced hammer may help then process along.

POWER UNIT

01.87 The only loose parts are the kickstart spring, which will probably fall out as the cases are parted, and this kickstart gear, which should be removed before it falls off later. Remember its orientation.

01.88 On pre-P series motors the cases can be more reluctant to split. If so, apply some heat around this raised area – it will help the bearing come free.

CRANK REMOVAL/INSPECTION

There is a special tool to press the crankshaft from the cases, but with care it can be tapped free without causing damage. A hot air gun with a cone attachment can be used to direct heat into the bearing inner race to assist the whole process.

Support the crank at the flywheel end during removal to keep it level as it's removed.

Once out, hold the crank firmly and pull the connecting rod back and forth, feeling for any play in the big end bearing. Side play is normal. Complete replacements can be found for most models, or possibly just a conrod kit, although the latter may not save much money once a machine shop has been paid to fit it. Check the side of the crank flywheels for scoring and any corresponding marks in the crankcase. The crank will need checking for alignment, which is best done at an engineering shop.

01.89 To get the crankshaft out, screw the clutch nut (or a similar threaded one) back on to the crank.

01.91 Once the crank is out, check the taper and threads for grooving or other wear. Make sure that the woodruff key slot is good.

01.90 Use a soft-faced hammer and drive the crank out of the case. If it doesn't move easily, try to get some heat into the bearing inner race and try again. On older engines the case may need to be heated to allow the bearing to come free along with the crank. They can be separated later.

HOW TO RESTORE CLASSIC LARGEFRAME VESPA SCOOTERS

01.92 The inner race of the flywheel bearing will stay on the crank (PX models). Note the gap between the race and the crank web. Measure it now if you don't have the correct shim tool.

01.93 The crank bearings are both large on pre-P series engines. Removal and replacement are dealt with later.

01.94 The drive-side crank oil seal can be removed. Carefully prise it free and discard. Seals should be replaced each time the cases are split.

XMAS TREE REMOVAL

This assembly is the input shaft mechanism, but is more commonly referred to as the Xmas tree. It incorporates the cush drive system, and is held to the case with a 13mm nut.

01.95 The primary drive unit can now come off. It is held by this nut – push down the tab of the lock washer and unscrew.

01.96 Under the nut is a specially-shaped washer and the locking tab. If it is re-useable, keep it safe.

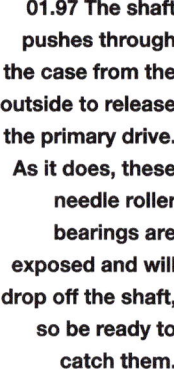

01.97 The shaft pushes through the case from the outside to release the primary drive. As it does, these needle roller bearings are exposed and will drop off the shaft, so be ready to catch them.

GEARBOX REMOVAL

01.98. The output shaft can be removed next. Use a soft-faced hammer on the end of the shaft – it should move relatively easily.

POWER UNIT

01.99 If you have a tight one – and internal seal late PXs are the worst – then use a metal drift, which fits neatly into the recess at the end of the shaft. Use a standard hammer to get things moving.

KICKSTART REMOVAL

The kickstart ratchet teeth should be checked for wear, along with the corresponding cog on the input gear cluster (Xmas tree). Replace if there is any doubt about the condition of either.

01.100 The final thing to remove from the cases is the kickstart mechanism. Remove the lever – it simply unbolts and can be wiggled free of its splines on the shaft.

01.101 The spring end can be prised from its slot in the metal pressing, the spring removed, and the shaft pushed through the case from the outside.

01.102 The whole assembly comes away like this.

BEARING REMOVAL FROM THE CASES

All the bearings in the crankcase can be driven out using a suitable drift, such as an old socket acting on the inner race. Heat the cases slightly to reduce the stress on them. Removed bearings cannot be re-used, and should be regarded as automatic replacements during a rebuild.

01.103 The clutch side main bearing is held by a circlip. Remove the clip and turn the case over.

01.104 If it is an earlier engine it too has a circlip, but it does not need to be removed. The bearing and seal can be taken out without disturbing it.

27

HOW TO RESTORE CLASSIC LARGEFRAME VESPA SCOOTERS

01.105 The bearing is driven out from this side – the alloy protrusions make sure of that.

01.106 Use a socket that fits the inner race size well. Gently heating the area around the bearing is good practice, as it relieves stress on the alloy during removal. The same method is used to drive the old-style bearing out of the case – it might also be tight, so heat the cases to assist removal.

01.107 The flywheel bearing is a needle-type on the P series.

01.108 It sits on a shoulder in the case so has to be removed from this side.

01.109 Use the same method on the clutch side. The drift has to be a good fit on this side as there is less of the bearing available to rest against. Heat the cases once again.

01.110 Remove the output shaft seal if you didn't do it earlier. Late PXs have a dust seal, as mentioned before.

POWER UNIT

01.111 There is a circlip underneath that also needs to come out.

01.112 The bearing has to be driven out from the inside, which requires a longer drift and some careful hammer swinging.

01.113 If the engine has the internal seal (arrowed) it has to be prised out after the bearing has been removed.

01.114 The selector box bearing is partly obscured by a casting, so obviously it has to be removed from this side. There is a special drift available, but careful use of a slim chisel tapped around the edge will work.

01.115 Heating the cases is always a good option to assist any bearing removal, but the selector box side is the best candidate for assistance, thanks to the restricted access for a drift.

01.116 On very early VBB type engines the output shaft bearing is a four-piece setup like this.

01.117 They're tricky to get out, thanks to a limited amount of lip to get a drift up against. They also pretty tight. Once out their construction is clear.

CASE CLEANING AND INSPECTION

If the rotary pad and the bearing seats are sound, the final place to check is around the rear shock absorber mount – if the scooter

01.118 It is a good idea to thoroughly degrease the cases – it will allow proper inspection before starting reassembly.

has had a hard life the cases can crack here. Once certain that all is well, the cases can be cleaned by vapour blasting if a perfect finish is required, and finished off with a high-temperature lacquer for longevity. If the budget doesn't stretch to that and the cases are heavily stained, a light coat of Simoniz crankcase paint or similar may be a suitable alternative.

01.119 A power washer comes in handy for rinsing off. When cleaning the cases, pay particular attention to any drillings, as they can become clogged with carbon.

HOW TO RESTORE CLASSIC LARGEFRAME VESPA SCOOTERS

01.121 Check the clean cases for signs of damage, especially around the rotary pad – any heavy scoring here will mean the cases are scrap. Although repair is possible through alloy welding and re-machining, it is easier and quicker simply to get another set.

01.122 Check the bearing recesses for damage or any cracking to the cases.

01.123 Check the mating surfaces of the cases for damage, and remove any traces of old gaskets or sealant.

BEARING REPLACEMENT IN CASES

Replacement bearings can be left in a plastic bag in the fridge overnight before fitting. The freezer can be used for a quicker cool down, but oil the bearings well and wrap them in a plastic bag to stop ice particles forming on them. This temperature reduction combined with some gentle heat applied to the cases will assist in fitting. Start the bearings off carefully making sure that they are square whilst going down, if not they will tighten quickly and can cause damage to the case if excessive force is used to seat them.

01.124 New crank bearings are available loose or as a kit with seals, as shown here. Buy your bearings from a reputable supplier and be very wary of good brands offered at a low price on the web – counterfeiting is a big problem.

01.125 The drive side (clutch) bearing is large. Special drifts are reasonably priced and make fitting much easier.

01.127 Once the bearing is down, refit the circlip to secure it.

01.128 Use good quality oil seals. Genuine ones are not much more expensive than copies.

01.126 Heat the case then drive the bearing into place, turning the case over as it nears its final position to check how close it is to the castings on the rear, which can be broken if you just keep pounding away. A seal driver can do the job nearly as well as the dedicated tool. If you don't have either, the bearing will have to be seated with a socket worked around the outer race, tapping the edge as you move. This last method – although perfectly feasible – is definitely the trickiest.

POWER UNIT

01.129 Push the seal home, making sure that it is square in the hole. It can be tight.

01.130 The flywheel bearing is a needle roller with a shallow shoulder, and is less robust than the ball roller on the other side of the crank. It is essential that you use a drift that matches the outside dimensions as closely as possible. There is a special tool that is fairly cheap and obviously designed for the job – a worthwhile investment if you think you will end up doing more than one rebuild.

01.131 The bearing sits on a clearly defined shoulder in the case.

01.132 Once again, warming the case first is a very good idea.

01.133 Once the bearing has been drifted into place, the oil seal can be fitted. It should be inserted until it is just flush with the casting. It can also be left until the crank is in place.

CRANKSHAFT BEARING REFITTING

01.134 To remove the inner race from a PX-type crank, cut a slot in it then another 180 degrees from that, making sure you do not cut through into the crank itself. Cover the rest of the crank with paper to prevent any debris getting into the big end bearing.

01.135 Heat the old race with a blow torch to expand it.

01.136 Use a chisel in the slots you cut to drive the old race off the crank. Wear eye protection, as bearing steel is brittle and can suddenly shatter.

HOW TO RESTORE CLASSIC LARGEFRAME VESPA SCOOTERS

01.137 To install the new inner race to the crank, it is essential that the crank web on that side is supported to stop twisting. One option is a wedge like this, which is cheap to buy.

01.138 The wedge taps into the gap in the crank webs to support them and prevent any tendency to close up when the new bearing ring is installed. The inner race has to be spaced from the crank and there is a special shim for this purpose (arrowed), although it is easy to fabricate one.

01.139 The new inner race has to be heated up to aid installation. A naked flame is fine as long as you do not overdo it, bearing steel is weakened by excessive heat, so only warm it up – do not allow it to change colour. A safer, if less rapid alternative, is to use a hot air gun.

01.140 The race should be fitted using this tool, again inexpensive, although an old Sundance alloy handlebar grip will do pretty much the same job.

01.141 With the crank wedge and spacer shim in place, quickly slide your warmed ring on to the crank. Using the correct drift, tap the race into place, using your body to absorb some of the shock.

01.142 Alternatively, put the crank in a vice and support the crank web with a couple of hefty spanners like this. That way the impact of installing the ring is only being applied to one web, so no twisting is likely to take place. This supported method is the one recommended by Piaggio.

01.143 On pre-PX cranks the bearings can stick on the crank rather than remain in the case as discussed earlier. A bearing splitter like this (although usually smaller) will be needed. The two halves of the tool are screwed together with a recessed lip squeezing behind the outer bearing race.

01.144 Two bolts and a puller plate are usually attached to draw off the bearing. Alternatively, place the whole lot over a vice, warm the bearing inner race, and tap the crank down and out of the bearing.

01.145 Replacement bearings are fitted, with the crank web supported on the side being worked on. Use a good fitting drift on the inner race to seat the bearing.

POWER UNIT

REFITTING CRANK

01.146 Before inserting the crank, grease the drive-side bearing to give it some lubrication on start-up, then grease the lip of the oil seal.

01.147 Push the crank by hand through the bearing. It will stop before going fully through, as seen here.

01.148 A crank installation tool can be bought, but a home made one is very easy to fabricate. Get a long bolt, washer and nut of a similar thread size to the crank end. Weld a clutch nut (arrowed) to the bolt head and you are ready to go.

01.149 The bolt minus nut and washer is screwed to the end of the crank. A spacer that matches the inner race of the bearing is slid into place followed by the washer and nut. Tightening the nut pulls the crank through the bearing, which is supported in precisely the right place to ease any strain on it.

01.150 Once the crank is home, check that the seal has not been caught during installation. A small section can be viewed through the arrowed cutout, so just turn the crank and inspect it all.

CUSH DRIVE OVERHAUL

The securing nut holding the assembly to the cases is torqued to 22 to 25.5lb-ft.

01.151 The 'Xmas tree' (layshaft) strip starts with the removal of this bearing. It is held in place by a circlip (arrowed).

HOW TO RESTORE CLASSIC LARGEFRAME VESPA SCOOTERS

01.152 Remove the clip, turn the tree over and tap the shaft down with a soft-faced hammer.

01.153 The shaft will come out with the bearing still attached.

01.154 Support the bearing between two bits of wood or in the open jaws of a vice, and put the nut back on the threads (slightly proud) to protect them. Tap down and the shaft will be released from the bearing.

01.155 Inside the large cog there are springs that provide cushioning on taking up drive. Two plates are riveted in place, trapping the springs. The rivets can be drilled out, but it is easier if you grind the heads flush first.

01.156 In theory the rivet bodies can then be punched through – in reality, some drilling will probably be required. The remains will usually then submit to a well-aimed punch.

01.157 The springs can be levered out using a screwdriver.

POWER UNIT

01.158 The cush drive then separates into the outer drive ring and the inner gear cluster.

01.159 The repair kit comes with two new plates, a set of large springs (PX 125 and 150), a set of small springs (used inside the large ones for the PX 200), and a set of rivets.

01.160 The new springs lever into place the same way the old ones came out.

01.161 Once the springs are in place check that the new rivets fit through the holes and there are no left over bits from the old ones still in there.

01.162 Tap over the head of the first rivet trapping the two plates with the underside supported on something solid. Do not fully tighten it down until the others have been lined up with their holes.

01.163 Pop the shaft back in place followed by the bearing which can be driven home using a suitable drift.

01.164 Replace the needle rollers using grease to hold them on to the shaft. Slide the shaft in just enough to hold the rollers: there should still be enough clearance to get the whole assembly in place and the shaft back through the hole in the cases.

HOW TO RESTORE CLASSIC LARGEFRAME VESPA SCOOTERS

GEARBOX STRIP AND INSPECTION

Before stripping the removed output shaft, measure the end-float – it should be 0.006 to 0.016in, and there are four different thrust washers available to achieve that figure. If any gears are replaced during the strip down, the shaft will have to be built again and the measurements taken once more to check the clearance is correct.

01.165 Refit the shaped washer, lock washer and nut. Make sure that none of the pieces overlap the clutch cover lip, and once tight, bend back the lock washer tabs to secure the nut.

01.166 Before stripping the gearbox, measure the end float with a pair of feeler gauges.

01.167 Remove the circlip. It is a strong one, so a decent set of circlip pliers is needed. Be careful, or it will launch itself across the workshop.

01.168 Next remove the thrust washer.

01.169 As you remove the gears, thread a cable tie through each one in turn as they come off. This will ensure correct reassembly later.

01.170 Once secured, give them a bath in degreaser.

01.171 The cruciform can be removed next.

POWER UNIT

01.172 Hold the shaft in a vice, then, using a 17mm spanner, undo the selector rod. It is a left-hand thread, so you will turn the spanner as if you were doing up a normal fitting.

01.173 The rod will come out leaving the cruciform in place. If the scooter is a late PX (EFL and on), there will be semicircular cutouts in the body of the shaft (arrowed).

01.174 Pull the cruciform up until the legs line up with the cutouts. The cutouts allow the cruciform to be turned parallel to the slot in the axle ...

01.175 ... which allows it to be pulled free.

01.176 The bottom thrust washer can now be removed. On EFL boxes there is another circlip under it, on pre-EFL it is a solid casting. Check for ridging or grooving where the gears sit. If it's extensive, you will need a new shaft.

01.177 The wear on the old cruciform is easy to spot. This would eventually lead to poor gear selection and the scooter dropping out of gear under load.

HOW TO RESTORE CLASSIC LARGEFRAME VESPA SCOOTERS

01.178 Pre-EFL scooters had a cruciform with a more defined arch shape and rounded legs.

01.179 It is removed and fitted using the rounded section of its own construction rather than cutouts in the axle, but the idea is essentially the same.

01.180 There is no washer between the selector rod and the cruciform on EFL scooters, or later. All others have one.

01.181 Clean the threads of the selector rod and add a little stud lock before fitting.

01.182 Before putting the gears back in place check the teeth for damage – normally either chips or grooves worn into them. Check too for pockmarks in the teeth, which would indicate that the case hardening is wearing off.

01.183 Check the slots (arrowed) where the cruciform contacts the gears too. The edges round off, and if badly worn will need replacing.

01.184 Check the threads, bearing surface, and splines of the shaft. This one is showing evidence of heat where the bearing sits (arrowed).

POWER UNIT

01.185 The output shaft bearing has to be refitted. If the engine is the internal seal type, the seal has to be pushed down and seated before the bearing is driven in. Refit the circlip or bearing retaining ring and seal.

01.186 Refitting the shaft is straightforward, but requires care. Use a deep drift that comfortably sits over and clear of the back of the selector rod, resting on the steel of the shaft only. Tap the shaft through the bearing; if it is reluctant, spin the gears a little as you go, which will encourage them to line up.

REASSEMBLY OF CASES

Just as during disassembly, the right-hand case will be fitted to the left-hand one. Pre-PX motors should have the main bearings mounted on the crank. The right-hand case may need gentle heating around the main bearing area to allow it to be pushed into place. The case studs should be fitted with a flat washer, then a spring washer, then the nut. They should be tightened progressively to avoid any distorting forces being applied. Once tight, it is good practice to check that the crank moves freely.

01.187 With the gears, Xmas tree, and crank back in, the left-hand case is pretty much done, so attention can be turned to the flywheel half.

01.188 There is an oil seal hiding inside the kickstart shaft hole. A slim pointed pick will be needed to get it out. The new seal should be greased then rolled down the hole and into position using your finger.

HOW TO RESTORE CLASSIC LARGEFRAME VESPA SCOOTERS

01.189 The old kickstart rubbers should slide out of the case. Once out they can often look much worse, so always change them as they are very cheap.

01.190 Push the kickstart shaft through and insert the straight part of the spring into the crankcase hole. The spring then needs to be turned until it sits inside the steel pressing again. It is strong, so be careful when levering it.

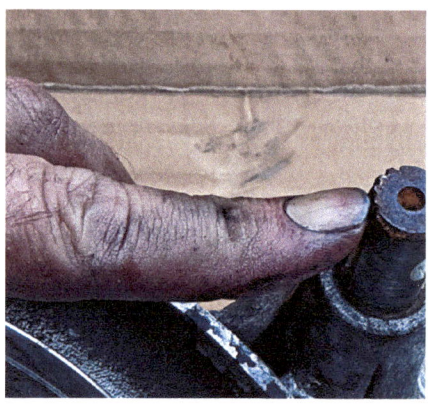

01.191 The kickstart lever and shaft have matching splines, and these are not interchangeable between model ranges. For example, a VBB lever will not sit correctly on PX splines.

01.192 Aftermarket kickstarts are made with altered splines, so this curved Sprint style kickstart is actually fitted to a PX engine, giving the scooter the correct retro look.

01.193 The selector box bearing needs fitting. Once again a tool is available, but a socket can be used just as easily.

01.194 Apply a little grease to both the flywheel and the selector box bearing.

01.195 The kickstart spring is held in place with some grease too. Put the kickstart cog on the end of the Xmas tree.

POWER UNIT

01.196 Piaggio does not recommend any sealant between the case faces, but suggests a smear of grease ...

01.197 ... which helps to stick the case gasket in place. If the oil thrower (arrowed) was removed during case cleaning make sure that it is back in place before closing the case halves. On early models it was part of the case casting itself.

01.198 Slide the flywheel side on and gently tap with the heel of a hammer to seat it.

01.199 If it will not go all the way down easily, move the kickstart down slightly and it should all close up together. Fit the four case nuts in the middle, but don't tighten them fully just yet.

01.200 Grease the shaft of each bolt before fitting, especially the one by the oil hole as it is prone to rusting. Once they are all in, tighten them evenly then use a torque wrench to tighten the nuts inside the stator recess. The other case bolts should then be torqued.

CLUTCH OVERHAUL

Both types of largeframe Vespa clutch rely on steel and cork plates running in gearbox oil. It is a false economy to just replace the corks, as the metal plates also wear, and, although it may

HOW TO RESTORE CLASSIC LARGEFRAME VESPA SCOOTERS

be harder to detect, they also warp. The steel plates are slightly dished and must all face the same way – if they are mismatched the clutch will be snatchy and oil flow around the clutch will be compromised, leading to high wear rates. It is important when disassembling an old clutch that all the plates are laid out in order so they can be replaced as they came out, should they be reusable. Replacements should be kept in the same order as they are packaged. Cheap clutch components are definitely a false economy, especially on the early clutches, as they are snatch prone even when in perfect condition. The seven-spring clutch fitted to the 200cc/T5 engines is physically larger, and will not fit the smaller engines without first losing some of the crankcase casting in the clutch recess.

There are a variety of clutch upgrades on the market, from stronger springs to welded reinforced baskets, but none are necessary for engines in standard tune.

Old style clutch rebuild

On seven spring clutches there may be a small guide hole in the bottom plate/clutch centre. If there is, there should be a corresponding hole in the basket. Be sure to line them up when reassembling.

01.201 Up to the arrival of the Cosa variant, the clutch fitted to most of the production run looks like this, with six (125/150 engines) or seven (200 or T5 engines) distinctive spring cups visible.

01.202 Clutches are often described by the number of teeth – for example, a 21-tooth clutch. This can be checked by marking a starting point (here in white) then counting the teeth (arrowed). At the back of the clutch, check the condition of the woodruff key slot. If it is damaged or elongated the clutch centre is scrap.

01.203 To disassemble either type of clutch, this securing ring (arrowed) has to be removed.

01.204 A compressing tool will be required, although a long bolt and a couple of suitably sized washers makes an adequate substitute.

POWER UNIT

01.205 The large plate sits in the recess in the front of the clutch.

01.206 With the clutch compressed and the ring removed, the plates are accessible.

01.207 Take them out one at a time and lay them in order.

01.208 The old friction plates (corks) should be checked for wear, which is done by checking the depth of material left above the grooves cut into them. Check too for signs of blackening, or areas where the material seems to have been polished – both indicate overheating. The ears that sit in the clutch basket burr over as well. New plates are very cheap, and should be regarded as an automatic replacement item when stripped down. The metal plates should be changed at the same time as the corks.

01.209 The bottom plain plate is attached to the cog mechanism in the centre of the clutch, which can be lifted from the basket ...

01.210 ... leaving the rest of the assembly looking like this.

01.211 Undo and remove the compressing tool, which will allow the centre to lift up under pressure from the springs below.

01.212 Lift the centre away and the springs and their cups are exposed. The springs should be checked for height, and the cups for signs of wear and scoring.

01.213 There is a brass washer at the bottom of the central shaft (arrowed). It should be replaced after noting its orientation.

01.214 The larger brass bush (arrowed) pulls free, and unless it is absolutely perfect it too should be replaced straight away.

HOW TO RESTORE CLASSIC LARGEFRAME VESPA SCOOTERS

01.215 The edges of the basket (arrowed) should be examined for grooves worn into the sides of the plate slots. This would allow the clutch to chatter, and impede clean operation. Minor marking can be removed with a file, but anything deep will mean a new basket. Baskets also tend to spread with time, so check for any signs of ovality as you look at it square-on. Tuned engines may have an additional band welded around the basket to reinforce it.

01.216 Reassembly begins by fitting the springs and cups back into the basket, then slipping the centre assembly into place and fitting the compressing tool.

01.217 As it compresses, the springs will not automatically line up, so pop them into place with a thin screwdriver. They should click as they go.

01.218 New corks and steels can be bought as a set. Keep them in the same order as they came out of the packet. There may be loose debris in the slots of the friction material: clean it up if there is.

01.219 Soak the corks overnight in gear oil before fitting. Once the corks and steels have been replaced the securing ring needs to be put back. Make sure the open ends sit inside the basket.

Cosa clutch rebuild

01.220 The Cosa clutch has a smooth face with no cups.

01.221 Just like the early clutch the plates are held in place by a securing ring.

01.222 The same compressing tool is used.

01.223 The ring is levered from its recess.

01.224 Once again, the corks should be examined for wear and depth of friction material left at the grooves.

01.225 There are more plates than in the earlier clutches.

POWER UNIT

01.226 The bottom plate is loose on the Cosa clutch, unlike its predecessor.

01.227 The centre spider (on the left) pulls free from the basket ...

01.228 ... leaving this. Undo the compressing tool.

01.229 The springs sit underneath the central plate, and are located on short pegs.

01.230 There is a washer and bush (arrowed) just like the earlier clutch, but the washer is wider. Nonetheless it should still be automatically renewed. Make note of its orientation before removal.

01.231 Reassembly starts by compressing the centre once more. Lining up the cutouts (arrowed) takes some care.

45

HOW TO RESTORE CLASSIC LARGEFRAME VESPA SCOOTERS

01.232 New plates are gear oil soaked and fitted, just like on the older clutch outlined previously. Take note that the second to bottom metal plate has a notch (arrowed), so make sure it goes back in the right place.

01.233 The securing ring is fitted once more, making sure that the open ends sit inside the basket for maximum security.

01.234 There should be clearance between the clutch centre and the driven cog to prevent dragging. 2mm is the minimum.

CLUTCH REFITTING

Check and replace the woodruff key if it is showing signs of wear. The old style clutch with slotted nut is torqued to 29-32.5lb-ft. Some vendors sell a standard nut and shake-proof washer to replace it, which makes everything a lot easier. Cosa clutches are done up to the same torque. The clutch cover bolts, whether 8mm or 10mm, should be done up to between 11 and 14.5lb-ft.

01.235 Fit the clutch woodruff key back in the crank followed by the spacer – geared in this case, as it is an autolube scooter. Make sure that it meshes with the drive cog.

01.236 Next, insert the autolube driveshaft (if fitted).

01.237 Push the clutch assembly on to the crank and refit the washer and nut. Tighten to the correct torque.

01.238 The brass plunger in the clutch cover should be replaced if the central slot is worn or shows signs of distortion. This one is not bad. If it needs changing, simply turn the clutch operating lever and the bush pops out.

01.239 There is a large rubber O ring around the lip of the cover – remove it and replace.

01.240 The cover also includes this breather, which simply unscrews. Blow through it to check that it is clear.

POWER UNIT

REAR HUB REASSEMBLY

The rear hub nut should be torqued to 54 to 65lb-ft.

01.241 The rear hub backplate seals should be replaced. There is one large seal, one small, and a pair joined like spectacles.

01.242 The backplate pushes into place and is secured by the three self-tapping screws.

01.243 The rear hub seal can be replaced next. (Or the dust seal if a late scooter, although the metal dust seal can itself be junked in favour of an old-type rubber seal, if preferred.) Check the measurements of the old seal – there are two types: one is 27 x 47 x 6mm, and the later type (approximately after 1983, but there's a lot of crossover) is 30 x 47 x 6mm. The size is moulded into the seal itself.

01.244 If fitting new brake shoes, they may come with the metal end plates loose like these.

01.245 They sit just over the end of the shoe that sits on the actuating cam.

01.246 The ends can be tapped down with a pointed hammer to secure them or squeezed together with a pair of pliers.

01.247 The friction material may come already chamfered at the edge (arrowed): if not take a file and make your own.

01.248 Put some masking tape over the friction material before you try to fit the shoes, it will stop you getting oily fingermarks on them as you work.

01.249 Put a dab of copper grease on the pivot points to discourage future corrosion. To fit the shoes, put one in place completely, then start the pivot end of the other on its post, pulling down against the spring pressure until the shoe is over the edge of the cam. Tap both ends of the shoe evenly until it pops into place. Put the horseshoe clips back in place on the pivot posts.

HOW TO RESTORE CLASSIC LARGEFRAME VESPA SCOOTERS

01.250 Peel away the masking tape.

01.251 The rear drum can be refitted, but check the section where it passes through the seal carefully. Note the spiral groove in this one (arrowed) – it was very light, but enough to cause the oil leakage into the drum pictured earlier. There is enough leeway on the seal for minor marking to be dressed out with a file. If it is too heavy, a new drum will be needed. Make sure that you order the correct one for your model.

CARB REFITTING

01.252 The carb box can now be put back on. Carefully clean the area where it will sit to remove old sealant or muck.

01.253 If you wish to remove the autolube system (for example when fitting a late engine into an earlier scooter), the best method is to use a proper blanking plug like this to seal the driveshaft hole.

01.254 Apply a smear of gasket sealant around the edge of the plug and push it into place.

01.255 Apply sealant to the face of the case where the carb box will sit, followed by a gasket.

01.256 On autolube scooters the underside of the carb box contains the oil channel (arrowed) that feeds the carb. The box should be cleaned and if you decide on using sealant on this surface make sure that it does not and cannot obstruct this groove for obvious reasons.

POWER UNIT

01.257 Put the carb box in place and secure with this screw.

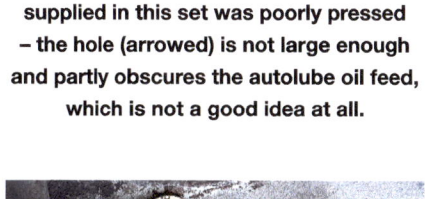

01.258 There is another gasket that the carburettor sits on. Unfortunately the one supplied in this set was poorly pressed – the hole (arrowed) is not large enough and partly obscures the autolube oil feed, which is not a good idea at all.

01.259 A better quality one was sourced, which had a generous cut around the oil hole.

FLYWHEEL REFITTING

With a clean but ungreased or oiled taper, the flywheel nut should be torqued to 43-47lb-ft.

01.260 Replacing the stator is straightforward. Slip the wires through the hole in the casting, then line up the ignition timing marks and screw into place. Fit the woodruff key to the crank, slip on the flywheel, followed by the crinkly washer, and tighten the securing nut.

TOP END REASSEMBLY

The piston has an arrow on the crown – make sure that it points toward the exhaust port. Lubricate the bore and rings well. Compressing the rings by hand as the piston is inserted is usually possible, but if that proves tricky use a ring compressing tool and fit the piston into the bore before sliding it all down over the studs to meet the conrod. Always support the piston whilst fitting the gudgeon pin; heating the piston slightly will aid fitting.

There is no head gasket so the sealing ring has to be clean and flat.

The cylinder head nuts should be tightened in a diagonal sequence, ending with a torque of 9.5-13lb-ft for 125/150 motors, and 12-16lb-ft for 200cc versions.

01.261 Make sure that the cases are clean where the cylinder base gasket will sit. If the studs have been removed or replaced, use some thread-locking compound to hold them in place.

HOW TO RESTORE CLASSIC LARGEFRAME VESPA SCOOTERS

01.262 Apply sealant to the case, as this is a leak-prone area. Slide the base gasket into place; they are usually paper.

01.263 Grease the stud shanks to prevent corrosion build-up.

01.264 Soak the little end in some two-stroke oil and slide into the crank.

01.265 If you are re-using the original piston, thoroughly clean out the ring grooves before fitting new rings. Use an old ring broken in half as a scraper, but don't be too rough with it which will gouge the piston groove.

01.266 The rings are going to sit against these locating pins which stops them rotating and catching in the ports. Make sure the pins are there and not loose.

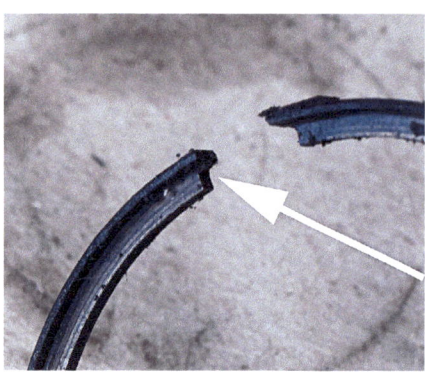

01.267 The rings have cutouts to match the locating pins. This ring is from a late EFL PX and is L-shaped. The upright section (arrowed) faces up towards the crown.

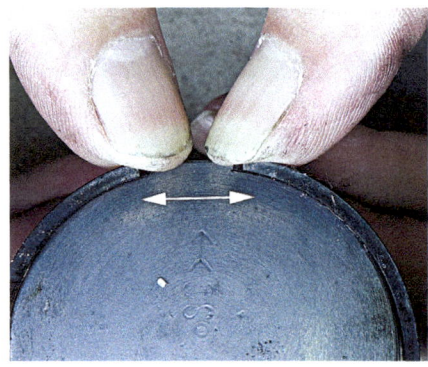

01.268 Rings have to be spread open to get them into place. They are brittle, so care must be taken to apply force evenly and gently.

01.269 Either hone the bore with the appropriate tool or use a piece of rough paper to clean and rough up the surface slightly. Clean the top of the cylinder where the head will sit.

01.270 Put the new rings in your cleaned or honed bore and first of all check that there is a ring gap (arrowed).

POWER UNIT

01.271 Use the piston to make sure that the rings are sitting squarely in the bore, and push them in approximately 20mm. Once they are square, use feeler gauges to measure the exact size of the gap (arrowed), which should be 0.010 to 0.016 inches (0.25 to 0.4mm). If it is too small use a file on the ends of the ring until the correct tolerance is achieved.

01.272 Fit the rings and insert the piston in the bottom of the bore, squeezing and compressing the rings to get them to fit. Alternatively, use a ring compressing tool. Align the piston with the small end of the crank, and push in the gudgeon pin. Often this is tight, so a little heat will persuade it to move. Use a screwdriver or similar – not your fingers – to push it into place once it is hot.

01.273 The cylinder head should be clean and free from carbon, and the sealing ring (arrowed) undamaged and level.

01.274 The head is secured by a flat washer followed by a spring washer, then the nut on each stud. Use a torque wrench, and secure the nuts in a diagonal sequence. The shroud securing sleeve needs to be refitted to the upper right-hand stud. Refit the cowl, sparkplug and cap.

SELECTOR BOX

New selector boxes are available for most of the models covered by this book. However, the quality can be patchy, with even genuine parts suffering the odd problem. PX EFL boxes differ from the Mark 1 PX (pre-1984) with the selector pawl resting at a different position for each gear, and with different notching on the selector disc. The two are physically interchangeable, but gear selection will be severely compromised. There are new boxes on sale which supposedly cover

01.275 The selector box should be cleaned and inspected for wear at the pivot (arrowed). Both the arm and the central pin are prone to wear.

51

HOW TO RESTORE CLASSIC LARGEFRAME VESPA SCOOTERS

01.276 Inside the box the pivoting guide (right-hand arrow) can wear. The arm is secured by a pin (left-hand arrow) but it is difficult to get out.

01.277 The guide is slid into the end of the selector rod, which is fiddly, then the whole assembly pushed flush to the case and the securing nuts fitted.

both models and are meant to work, but owner feedback seems thin on the ground at the time of writing. Refitting the box is tricky as the gearbox selector rod needs to be fully out, then the pivoting square end of the selector lever slid between the grooves whilst simultaneously lining up the holes over the studs before pushing it all down into place.

ENGINE MOUNT REPLACEMENT

The PX type of front mount is shown in the pictures. The earlier version has a solid hollow shaft rather than being split, but the principle of removal and replacement is the same, just more awkward, as they tend to seize in place more frequently.

01.278 Check the rear shock mount for signs of wear or deformation: usually the sleeve sags from the centre of the bush when worn.

01.279 The easiest way to remove the old bush is to make up a simple puller arrangement. The socket on the left is larger than the bush, the spacer on the right the same size. As the nut is tightened towards the arrow, the bush is forced out.

01.280 Once it is moving it should be simple to push it all the way out. If it is still tight and has reached the limit of the socket, use a deeper one to give yourself the necessary reach.

01.281 With the bush removed the full extent of the wear can be seen.

01.282 Make sure the hole in the case is clean before attempting to renew the bush. Reverse the process above to reassemble. The new bush will be tight, so you may have to insert the rubber without the steel tube, then use the tool to insert the tube. Either way, lubricate with a little hand soap or rubber grease to encourage movement.

POWER UNIT

01.283 On PXs, if you look inside the cutout of the casting where the main pivot bolt passes through, two tubes can be seen.

01.284 Using a strong screwdriver lever apart the tubes (arrowed).

01.285 Hopefully, you will be able to pull the first one out of the casing a fair way. Get a pair of grips on it and pull it out.

01.286 A long drift can then be used on the other to drive it out of the case.

01.287 Underneath each rubber there should be a metal shim, which may be corroded.

01.288 Before fitting the new bushes make sure that the alloy seat is clean.

HOW TO RESTORE CLASSIC LARGEFRAME VESPA SCOOTERS

01.289 Make a puller from some threaded bar, nuts and suitably-sized washers. Lubricate the rubber before fitting.

01.290 Use the central tube initially to start the seating process.

01.291 The bush may stick before it is fully home, and the natural spring of the rubber may dissipate the force used to try and insert it. If that is the case, stop using the metal tube, and try a large diameter socket resting on the outside edge of the rubber. It should get the last bit in.

01.292 The new bush should be very slightly proud of the case when seated as the front face is slightly chamfered.

01.293 Models before the P series had a one-piece tube which is trickier to get out and refit.

01.294 This type can resist all efforts with a puller, so to encourage movement you may have to drill some holes around the edge to loosen the grip of the bush. This technique can be used on reluctant P series bushes too.

01.295 The old rubbers may just break up rather than come out. A blow lamp may be useful to get rid of stubborn remains. The steel tube may still be reluctant to move – try lubrication and heat. If these fail, take it to an engineering shop to have it pressed out. Bush refitting is the same process as the P series outlined above, using a selection of spacers and a threaded bar to apply the necessary force to insert the parts.

REFITTING ENGINE

Make sure that the rear shock absorber and any cables are well out of the way, then lift the front of the engine unit and slide the well-greased pivot pin through. It might take a little jiggling to get started and once again as it exits the other side of the frame, but once in, the rear of the engine can be lifted and the shock absorber bottom bolt slid into place. The main pivot pin nut should be tightened to 44-54lb-ft. The rear shock nut to 16.5-18.5lb-ft. Reconnect all the cables and fuel lines. The oil feed is impossible to attach without leaving an air bubble in the line but that will prove advantageous later. Fill the gearbox with oil until it flows out of the filler hole which also acts as a level indicator.

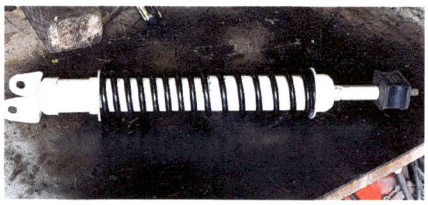

01.296 Refit the shock absorber if it has been removed, along with a new mounting block at the top, as they sag and split with age. Genuine parts are strongest.

POWER UNIT

01.297 Make sure that any wiring and cables are taped out of the way before starting.

01.298 The back end of the frame needs to be supported. Make sure that the main pivot bolt is well greased before fitting. It should go in first, then the engine pivoted up and the shock bolt fitted.

01.299 The cables can then be threaded back into their adjusting sleeves and the trunnions refitted, or even better, replaced. The small metal discs shown sit on top of the cable, between it and the securing bolt, to prevent the latter cutting the cables. The rear brake cable uses a nut clamping a plate.

01.300 With the gearbox and handlebar in neutral, the cables can be tensioned with dedicated pliers or with a standard set and the trunnion bolts tightened. A final adjustment will probably be necessary once the scooter has been on the road for a few miles, especially if new cables have been fitted.

01.301 Make sure that the exhaust bolt is well greased too, as these seize in the case and are very tricky to drill out.

01.302 Replace any damaged rubbers, such as the intake tube.

01.303 Fit new washers to the drain and level plugs.

HOW TO RESTORE CLASSIC LARGEFRAME VESPA SCOOTERS

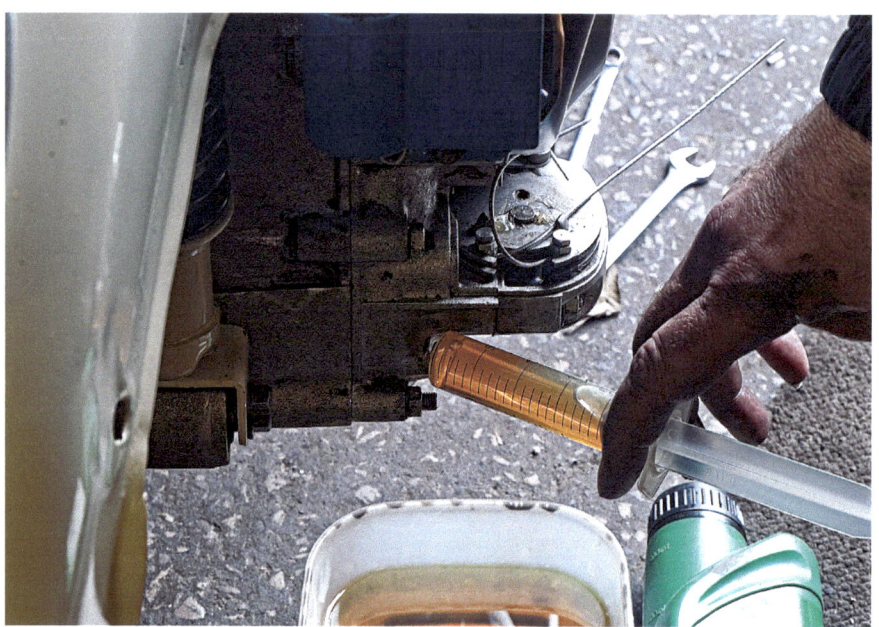

01.304 A syringe is perfect for refilling the gearbox. Scooter shops sell them, but I prefer the smaller ones, which are also a lot cheaper. Just keep filling until the oil starts to flow back out. Leave it until the drips have stopped, then refit the level plug.

STARTING UP

If the scooter has autolube it will take a short time for the oil line to bleed itself, so add a 2 per cent mix (50:1 ratio) to 3 litres of petrol in the tank before starting. Pre-mix scooters obviously do not need this precaution. Start as normal, but do not rev the engine much – allow it to tick over a soon as it is willing. Have a look at the oil feed line – the air bubble should be moving towards the engine, which indicates that the pump is working. Check for leaks of fuel or oil, and wait for the excess oil and greases used during assembly to burn off. Running-in should be a minimum of 500 miles, with a light load put on the engine rather than depending on a rigid throttle position. After 1000 miles slacken and re-torque the cylinder head nuts, and check the other fixings for security.

Chapter 2
Fuel & exhaust

FUEL TANK REMOVAL/ INSPECTION

Regardless of model, all the tanks are held in place by bolts in captive nuts in the frame, or by a plate bridging the frame. The fuel tap lever needs to be turned so the tab is pointing directly up to enable removal. The rear of the tank should be lifted first and the assembly kept at an angle until the lever and autolube sight glass (if fitted) are clear of their respective holes. The tank can then be rested on the edge of the frame whilst the fuel line clip is released, having first ensured that the tap is back in the off position.

Once drained of any remaining fuel the tank should be checked for internal corrosion. Light surface rusting is not a problem, but blistering scabby stuff most definitely is. Tank sealant can be used to coat the inside, but make sure that it is resistant to ethanol, which is being used increasingly in modern fuels. If the tank is beyond repair copies are available, and although there may not be an exact match for your particular model, there will be one that fits.

To replace, simply reverse the removal process. If it proves difficult to line up the lever to get it back

02.1 The fuel tank is held in by bolts at the rear and the seat hinge at the front. This is an early largeframe type – the fixings are obvious and similar across all models and years.

02.2 If a fuel gauge is fitted, the connector for the wiring is under a grommet, which once peeled free of the frame allows the connector to be pulled up and then separated.

02.3 The seal around the fuel tap lever needs to be removed. It's easier for the moment just to push it back into the frame with a screwdriver, and remove it later. Turn the tap so the lever tab is pointing upwards.

57

HOW TO RESTORE CLASSIC LARGEFRAME VESPA SCOOTERS

02.4 Lift the tank straight up, then tilt the rear upwards and pull back slightly as you lift it away. This gets the lever out of the frame hole.

02.5 Under the tank is a rubber or nylon seal, depending on year. Remove and examine it for signs of deterioration. Don't forget to put it back before the tank goes in.

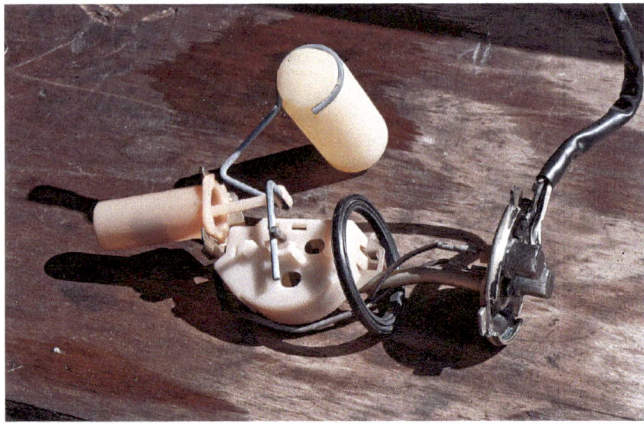

02.6 The fuel gauge sender unit is held by a locking ring, which taps round to release the unit. If it is faulty, substitution is the only real answer.

02.7 If you have an autolube scooter then the oil tank sits underneath the petrol tank. The PX type is plastic and can be removed. Previous versions, which are much rarer, have metal units permanently attached to the tank.

02.8 Removal of the autolube tank starts by undoing this plastic ring.

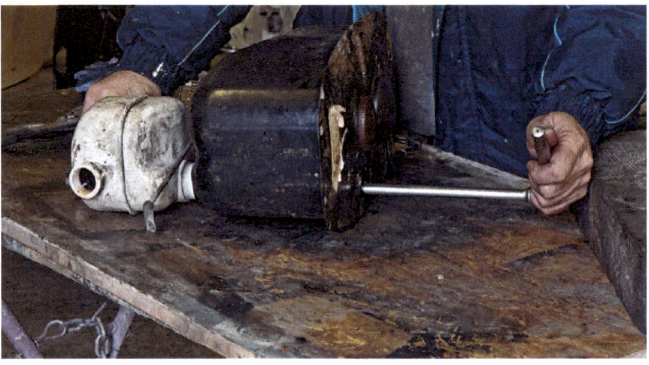

02.9 The main oil tank securing nut is deep inside the tube that the oil passes down. It needs a 17mm socket on a long extension to get it off. Hold the outlet nut at the bottom with a spanner.

FUEL & EXHAUST

02.10 Once undone, the outlet nut comes free. Replace the seal on the bottom unless it is perfect.

02.11 There is another seal (arrowed) under the top cap. Once again, inspect and replace as necessary.

02.12 The sight glass is plastic – there is a seal between it and the tank (arrowed). This unit is prone to hairline cracking, so examine it closely before re-use. Replacements are cheap.

When refitting, slide the nut down the copper tubing and use a screwdriver to get it started on the thread, then revert to the special tool when things start to get tighter. Make sure the tap is pointing in the right direction to allow the lever to be fitted, and get the tank back in the frame.

The fuel pipe should be automatically changed during any restoration. Measure the old one and cut the new to the exact length. It is tempting to add a little bit more, which makes refitting the tank easier, but it may result in air locking as there is not much room in the body cavity, and the extra length may coil upwards and reduce flow when the tank is low.

02.14 The tap washer is accessed by undoing two screws that secure a plate as seen in the last photo, and removing the alloy casting underneath. A new seal should be used every time the tap is opened.

through the frame hole, as it can wobble around, tape some wire to it, feed the wire through first, and use that to pull the lever into position. The rubber washer that sits around the oil sight glass should be fitted first, and the inner edge lightly lubricated.

FUEL TAP AND LINE

Replacement tap assemblies are readily available, and if you are willing to do without the sediment bowl, for example, they are also very cheap. Removal of the tap assembly is straightforward – the only potential problem may be a tight retaining nut, in which case hold the tap with a set of self-locking pliers to stop it turning until the nut is loosened.

02.13 The operating lever is held to the fuel tap body by an R clip.

02.15 Early scooters (approximately pre-1970) had a sediment bowl built in; metal in this case, but also in glass. Unscrew the knurled nut and pivot the assembly out of the way. The bowl then pulls down from the tap.

HOW TO RESTORE CLASSIC LARGEFRAME VESPA SCOOTERS

02.16 The bowl system is very efficient. This one came from a scooter that had been running until it was traded in.

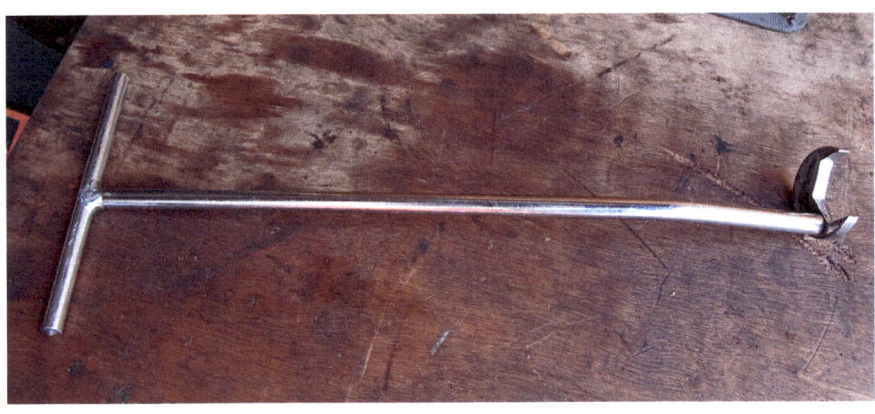

02.17 The tap assembly can only be removed by using a special cranked spanner.

02.18 Unfortunately the tools are often cheaply made. As supplied, this one did not fit the nut (the jaws were not wide enough), so some work with a file was needed before it was any use.

02.19 The filter arrangement on older taps is different to the later type. If a tap is to be re-used, the mesh screens and the tube within must be carefully inspected and cleaned.

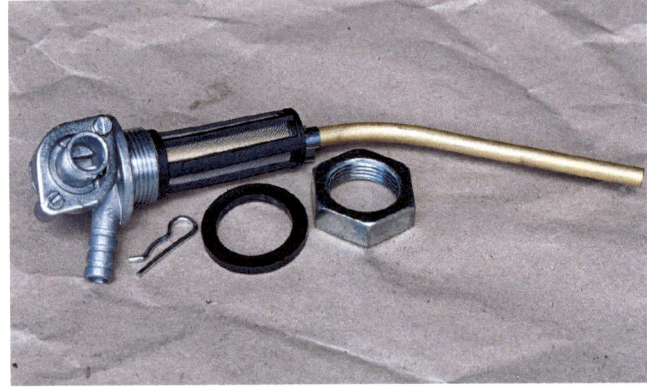

02.20 This is the type of tap most commonly found on sale now, and it is interchangeable across all models. It is possible to buy versions with or without a reserve position. They are inexpensive, so should really be an automatic swap on any rebuilt scooter.

02.21 When refitting the fuel line to the tap (or the autolube line) heat the end in some boiling water to soften it first – it makes the job much easier.

FUEL & EXHAUST

CARB STRIP/OVERHAUL

All the models covered by this book use a variant of the Dell'Orto SI series of carb. These all follow the same layout, although the earliest VBB era scooters may have a flap in the air box acting as a choke mechanism, rather than the carb-mounted plunger found on later versions (pictured).

02.22 All the rotary valve model carburettors have roughly the same layout and are interchangeable, as the mounting points remained the same throughout production. The inlet banjo may have been taken off already during the engine removal process – if not, unscrew it now, noting the large fibre washer next to the carb body and the small one under the bolt head. These washers should be replaced as a matter of course.

02.23 Under the top cover (sometimes referred to as the 'Chinaman's hat') is a seal that may come off with the top, or may stay attached to the body as here.

02.24 There is a mesh screen underneath. A slim pick may be needed to lift the edge and get it out.

02.25 There are two jets next to the cover. If it is a pre-80s carb then these may be obscured by a small plate, which is held by a single screw. The smaller one is the slow running jet and the larger is the main stack. They simply unscrew.

02.27 Jets should really only be blown through with compressed air. If you are faced with a stubborn bit of debris, a few strands of soft copper wire can be used to shift it. Replacement jets are inexpensive.

02.26 The sections of the main stack are: air corrector jet (white arrow), at the top with the screw slot used to get the assembly out; the middle section with the holes is the mixer tube (red arrow); and the small part at the end is the main jet (yellow arrow). All the sections have their sizes stamped into the metal for easy identification (if they are genuine parts, that is – some of the replacements made in the Far East are unstamped).

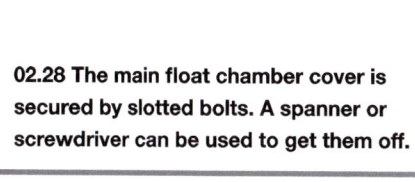

02.28 The main float chamber cover is secured by slotted bolts. A spanner or screwdriver can be used to get them off.

HOW TO RESTORE CLASSIC LARGEFRAME VESPA SCOOTERS

02.29 The lid lifts away, bringing the float assembly with it.

02.30 The starter jet is then accessible. It also unscrews.

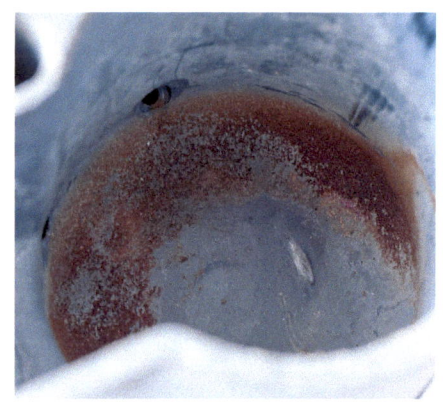

02.31 If the carb has been out of use for any length of time expect sediment in the bowl. This one is not bad, but often there is a hard yellowy/green crystalline deposit.

02.32 The float is held to the cast alloy post with a small pin. It needs to be pushed free with something suitably slim. Check the float for damage and shake it to make sure that there is no fuel in it. If it is holed it will have to be replaced.

02.33 The float needle can now be lifted free.

02.34 You can examine the tip, but wear can be difficult to judge, so just fit a new one with a red-coloured tip for unleaded petrol compatibility.

02.35 The throttle stop screw unscrews next. Count the number of turns it takes to get it out – it will give you a starting point when setting up the rebuilt carb.

02.36 The choke plunger is held by a single screw. The assembly just slides out once the screw is removed. It is a self-contained unit, and unlikely to give problems. Just check the end of the plunger for any signs of deep scoring or scuffing.

02.37 The throttle slide is held in by a plate secured by two screws. As the screws release their hold, the plate will push out under pressure from the internal spring.

FUEL & EXHAUST

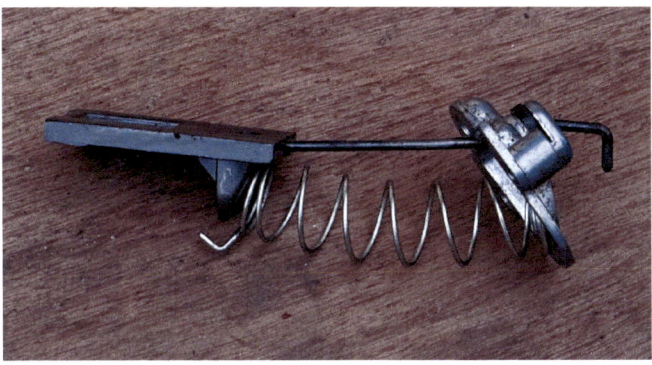

02.38 Note the position of the spring in relation to the operating rod for when you come to reassemble. There is a small seal where the rod passes through the cover – fish it out and replace.

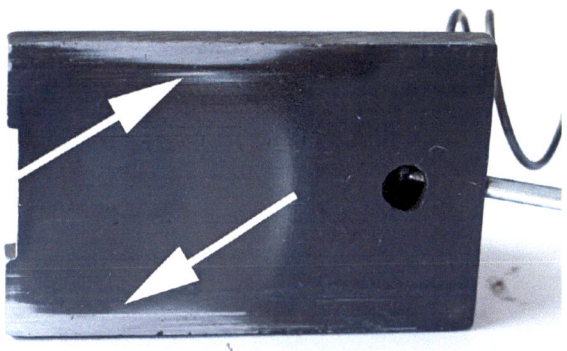

02.39 Check the slide for signs of wear. These marks were not deep, but shows how the surface can wear. If it has any grooving it needs to be replaced.

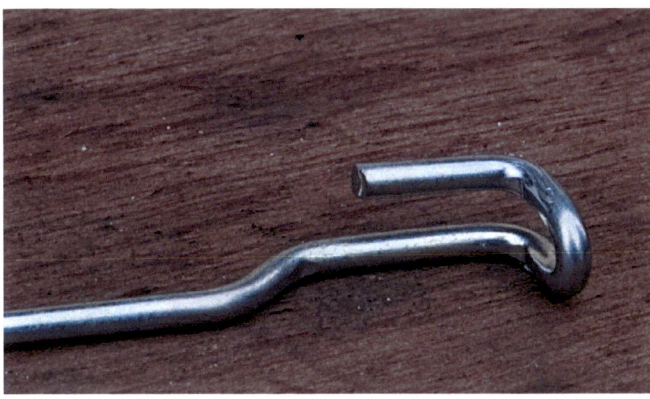

02.40 The slide operating rod has a different end depending on fitment. This one is for a pre-mix motor – if it had autolube the end would be a simple angled pin.

02.41 The final piece to remove is the mixture screw which also unscrews.

02.42 Once out, it looks like this. Check the tapered end (arrowed) for a wear lip or ridging.

02.43 With the carb completely stripped, degrease it thoroughly.

HOW TO RESTORE CLASSIC LARGEFRAME VESPA SCOOTERS

02.44 Give it a bath in a dedicated carb cleaner if there was a lot of sediment or gum in the float bowl. If the alloy is heavily discoloured, a short immersion in cellulose thinners will leave it looking like new. Be aware of the fire risk, though.

02.45 Blow through all passages and air drillings with compressed air (from a can if you do not have a compressor), and make sure all the threads are clean and dry.

02.46 If you are replacing a carb, check that the autolube holes are all present. There are some with the hole in the bottom flange, but not the drilling through to the other side of the slide.

02.47 Budget gasket sets might cut a few corners. This seal, for example, is rubber in a genuine set, but paper in the aftermarket version.

02.48 Don't cut corners on items like the filter – it will save you lots of hassle once on the road, as Vespa jets are small and block easily. Don't over-tighten the top cover either, as it is prone to leakage.

02.49 Clean, overhauled, and in this case converted for use on a pre-mix scooter, it should give several years of reliable service at low cost.

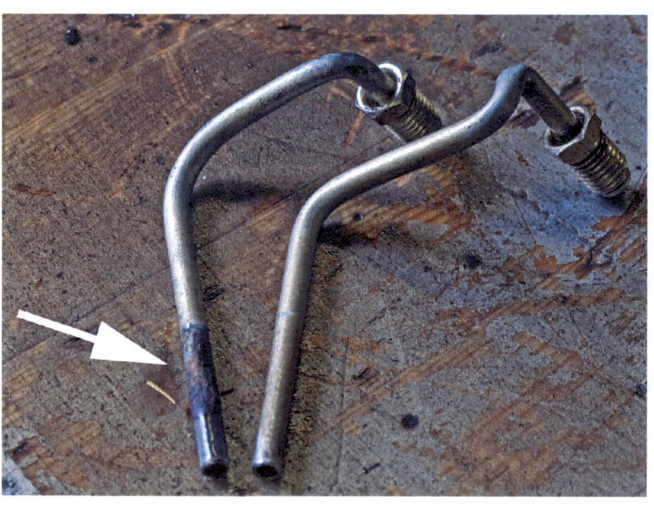

02.50 Check the autolube pipe where it runs into the carb box. It seems to corrode here, so replace before it starts leaking.

FUEL & EXHAUST

EXHAUST SYSTEM

Rust is the main enemy of the Vespa exhaust, and corrosion gets a grip quickly as paint coverage is not great. Blockages are possible, especially if the scooter has been sitting for some time when the old oily internal deposits start to solidify. A strong solution of caustic soda – used with extreme care and wearing eye and skin protection – can be used to dissolve this internal crud. Copies of the original exhausts are available new for virtually all models, and genuine Piaggio ones for the P series scooters. Performance enhancing pipes are a popular option, but many are not road legal, so check with the supplier first. A standard look with mildly enhanced performance can be achieved by fitting a Sito Plus or one of SIP's road versions with the main jet increased by a couple of points to suit. Some replacement pipes are a poor fit, and mounting brackets may have to be bent and holes opened up before they will go on.

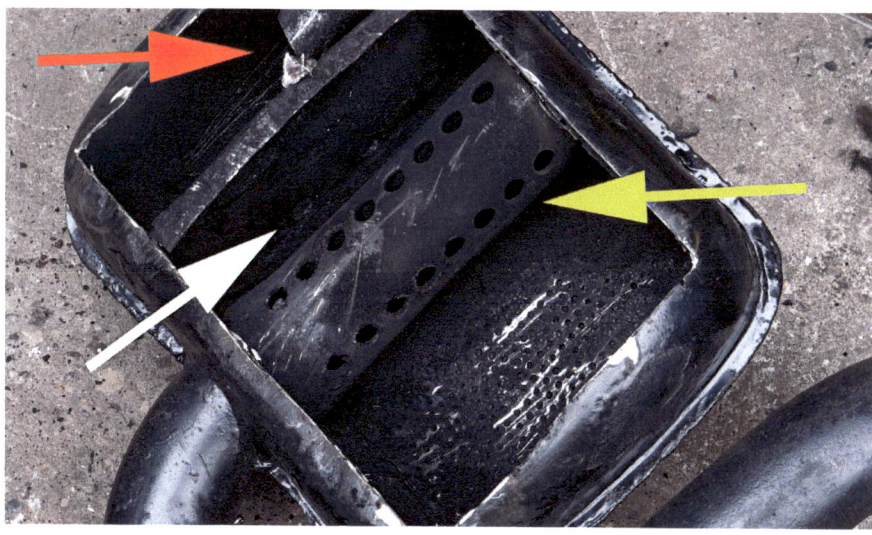

02.51 Standard exhausts are simple in construction and quite restrictive. The gas enters the main chamber through the large holes (yellow arrow). It then has to pass through a few much smaller holes (white arrow), into the second chamber. This restricts the flow and creates back pressure, which enhances torque. Finally the gases escape through the tail pipe (red arrow).

02.52 Aftermarket exhausts such as this Simonini are a popular choice when originality is not important, as they liberate a little more power. If the aftermarket option is attractive, make sure that your choice is road legal for your scooter. Many on sale are marked as not for road use.

Chapter 3
Front end

HEADSET STRIP EARLY

Pre-PX Vespa headsets are one-piece alloy castings, apart from a few rare VNB models with split pressed steel versions. They all have separate tubes for throttle and gear operation. Their construction is fairly simple, as we shall see, but you should note cable and wiring runs, plus the arrangement of any flat or wavy washers that sit on the tubes. It may seem obvious as it comes apart, but that may no longer be the case when it is time to put it all back together again. Check all parts that come into direct contact with cables – for example, the cable guide plate and the roller ends – for general wear or sharp edges.

03.1 The strip-down starts with headlamp removal. This is held in place by screws through the chrome outer ring.

03.2 The light should then pull free along with the rim, allowing the bulb holder at the back to be disconnected and the unit to be removed completely.

FRONT END

03.3 Inside the headset the cables should be clearly visible in their rollers. If you intend to keep all the old cables etc, they need to be released from their respective control levers, having undone the 'working' end at the front drum (and if the engine is still in, at the selector box and clutch operating lever as well). If the wiring loom is being re-used it needs to be disconnected from the handlebar switch. In most restorations, though, all of these items will be replaced, so they can be ignored for now.

03.4 The speedo is held by a long bolt accessed from the underside of the headset. Before undoing the knurled nut that secures the outer cable to the speedo head, wrap a little tape around the cable to prevent it slipping down inside the forks when released.

03.5 The headset should lift off the forks, but may need some gentle tapping upwards with a soft-faced hammer to encourage it. If you haven't undone all the cables and wiring, you should still be able to get the headset off and tilted back like this, which will allow you to cut through everything.

03.6 The handlebar lever pivot pins are secured by a locking nut on the underside. Once the nut is removed the pins screw out of the bars.

03.7 The best way to remove old grips is simply to slice them with a sharp knife and peel them off.

03.8 There should be removable plates under the head set. If they are there, and often they are not, unbolt them. Metal replacements are hard to track down if they are missing.

HOW TO RESTORE CLASSIC LARGEFRAME VESPA SCOOTERS

03.9 The light switch needs to come off, along with its wiring. Undo the middle screw and remove the lever, then wiggle off the chrome cover. It is a push fit, and the bottom plastic switch lever needs to be central to allow the cover to pull free.

03.10 The inner section of the switch assembly is held in place by another screw (arrowed), which needs to be undone.

03.11 The control tubes (arrowed), which are held together by spring clips, can be removed next. These can be levered out quite easily with a flat-bladed screwdriver.

03.12 The two sections of tube can then be separated – they simply pull apart.

03.13 The tubes may need cleaning before they can be pulled free. Once out, clean them thoroughly and check for ridging or other damage.

03.14 The headset is now bare and ready for cleaning and inspection.

68

FRONT END

03.15 Sheared bolts are common on the underside of the headset where the plates mount. To get the remains out, first drill a hole down the middle of the broken bolt.

03.16 Warm the casting around the stuck bolt. The alloy will expand quicker than the steel of the bolt, loosening its grip.

03.17 The old bolt should then unscrew with the help of a dedicated extractor.

03.18 Degrease the tubes ready for painting. If you don't plan to paint for some time, reassemble them and clip them back together, otherwise bits like this gear side washer can end up being lost. Make sure that the cable ends are not worn or have sharp edges, and check the cable guide plate whilst you are at it.

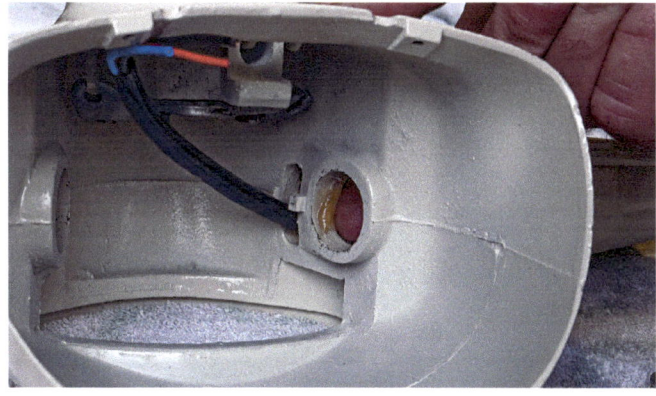

03.19 With the headset painted and ready for reassembly, fit the cable guide plate and the link wiring that runs to the switch.

03.20 Grease the tubes and the large washer on the gear side.

HOW TO RESTORE CLASSIC LARGEFRAME VESPA SCOOTERS

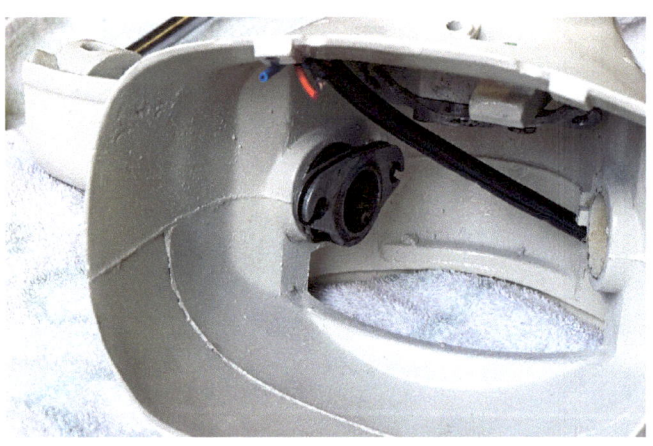

03.21 Grease the inner cable wheels where they pass through the alloy to discourage future corrosion.

03.22 Slide the two sections together and fit the retaining clip, which might need some guidance with a slim screwdriver to encourage the pin to line up with the bottom hole.

03.23 Do not forget the friction ring on the throttle side. It is held in place by the pivot bolt.

03.24 Place the headset loosely on the forks and start feeding the cables and loom into place.

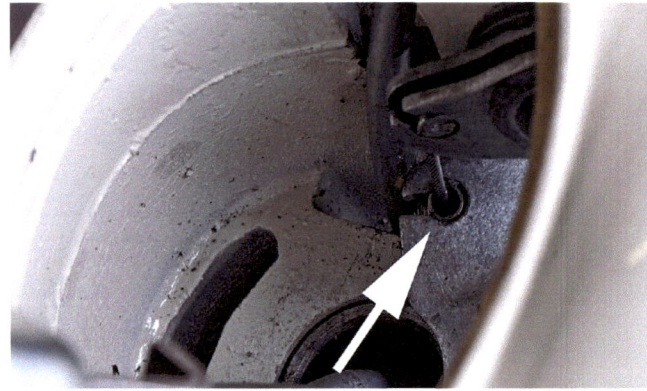

03.25 These cables came with metal top hats (arrowed) already fitted to the outer sleeves. If yours don't, remember to fit them before going any further. Check that the cables sit square to their holes and will not rub when operated.

03.26 Line up the headset with the front wheel so everything is pointing in the right direction, then gently tap it down with the heel of your hand. Insert the bolt through the groove in the forks then into the nut (arrowed), which is inserted from the underside. It will need to be held there with a fingertip until the bolt starts to screw in. Tighten to 22 to 31lb-ft.

FRONT END

03.27 Check the pivot points and cable attachments of the old levers; wear is common.

03.28 The cables insert by aligning them with the slot in the lever then twisting to the side. It's obvious when they are in your hand. Grease the pivot point well and insert a washer before sliding the lever in place and inserting the pivot bolt.

03.29 Headlight bulbs come in a variety of wattages, choose the right one for your scooter as the electrical system is marginal on older models. If you need a new bulb holder, buy a decent quality one as the connectors are poor on budget versions.

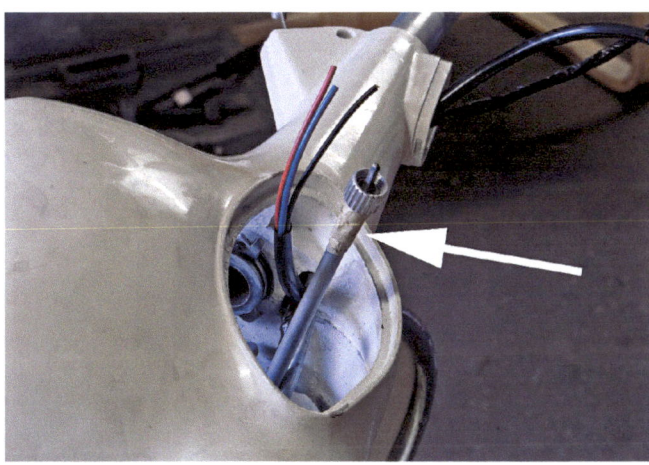

03.30 The speedo can be fitted now. Note the tape (arrowed) preventing the ferrule disappearing down the fork leg.

03.31 With some aftermarket speedos, clearance problems may occur due to the relative positions of the light connector and the securing plate. If so, some cutting work will be required (arrowed).

03.32 The light switch simply screws back in place once the wiring is connected to the rear. The connector holes are all numbered, or should be.

03.33 New grips can be lubricated with a little panel wipe or hair spray, then pushed on. If they tighten before going fully home, gently warm them with a hot air gun and apply a twisting motion as you push.

HOW TO RESTORE CLASSIC LARGEFRAME VESPA SCOOTERS

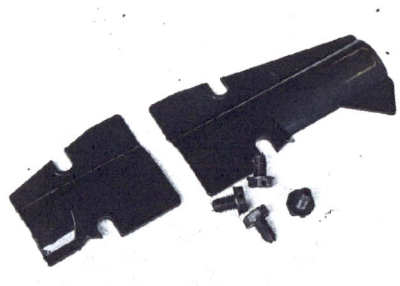

03.34 If the scooter is missing its underplates, plastic copies can be sourced – these came from Germany. Once painted, no-one is likely to notice that they are not metal.

03.35 The headlight can be fitted last to complete the job.

HEADSET STRIP PX

These headsets are much easier to work on than their predecessors, as they split, giving far greater access to all cables and wiring. Having said that, you'll still need to take notes.

03.36 The MkI PX has a round speedo with an ignition switch and warning lights mounted above.

03.37 The EFL speedo included the warning lights and a fuel gauge.

03.38 The disc models had an updated speedo, which is interchangeable with an EFL one as long as the wiring sub loom is changed at the same time.

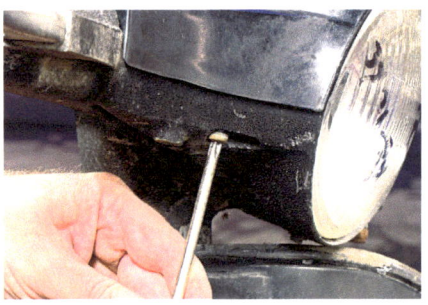

03.39 All versions have split headsets. The four securing screws are in recesses on the underside.

03.40 With the screws undone, push the speedo cable up from the fork bottom, which will lift the upper section of the headset.

FRONT END

03.41 The speedo cable on EFL models is held by a clip like this. Squeeze the legs together to free it. On pre-EFL models, the speedo cable is held by a knurled ring that unscrews. The ignition switch on the early models is best released by undoing the locking ring on the outside of the headset, and letting the whole assembly drop through with all the wiring still attached.

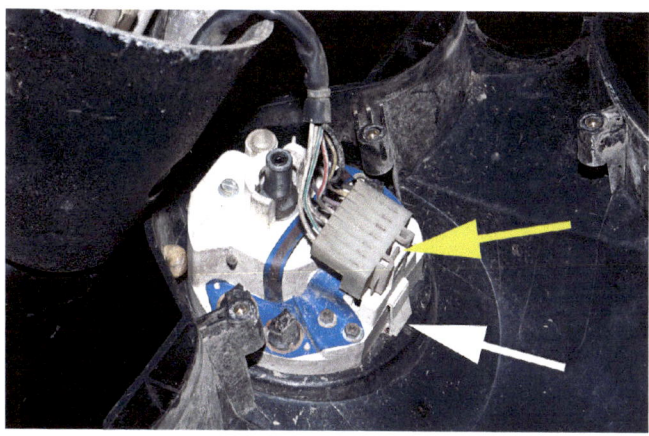

03.42 On the EFL models the wiring to the speedo just unplugs after pushing in this tag (yellow arrow) the speedo itself is freed by pushing in another tag (white arrow). MkI speedos are held in by a metal plate that is unscrewed.

03.43 With the top off, access to all components is good. Note the corrosion to the earth tag on the bulb holder, which is common.

03.44 Make a note of how the cables and electrics run. The headlamp is secured by a screw on each side (arrowed).

03.45 There should be one wavy washer on top of the lever and a plain washer underneath, but they seem to accumulate extra ones over the years. Note the amount of corrosion.

03.46 The clutch side has an extra switch (arrowed) built in on electric start models. It prevents the engine starting until the lever is pulled in. Don't bother trying to undo it unless it is faulty, just unplug the wire from the junction box behind the horn cast and pull it up and free.

HOW TO RESTORE CLASSIC LARGEFRAME VESPA SCOOTERS

03.47 The wiring multi plug looks like this. Trace the wiring down from the headset and unplug as necessary, then pull the wiring back up.

03.48 The headset securing bolt can be undone and the whole assembly lifted away, having either released the control cables or cut them.

03.49 The throttle and gear tubes have plastic end wheels where the cables attach. They are held in place by these metal clips.

03.50 The switches are secured by a single countersunk screw.

03.51 These particular tubes were corroded, as was the tunnel they pass through. Gentle heat was applied to the alloy, which eventually released its grip, assisted by a liberal application of releasing oil.

03.52 The headset tops are plastic, and although it is possible to fill or repair them it is simply uneconomic, as replacements are so cheap.

FRONT END

03.53 New tops come in a neutral colour. See the paint chapter for dealing with plastics.

03.54 Once the tubes have been cleaned and refitted, the plastic wheels can be reattached. Note the plastic top hats used by the PX (arrowed).

03.55 When you replace the wheels, don't forget the plain and wavy washers behind them.

03.56 Brake cables may come with these pear-shaped nipples (yellow arrow). Separate ends (white arrow) need to be threaded on to allow the cable to fit the lever.

03.57 Braking is not an area where parts quality should be an issue. Unfortunately, this brake lever broke under normal use in under 250 miles. Not good.

03.58 Grease the lever and fit a wavy washer on top and a plain one underneath, then slide the lever into place.

MASTER CYLINDER

The master cylinder should be checked for leaks and damage to the rubber dust seal. The main seals can be checked for operation before disassembly by pumping the lever and holding the pressure on. Gently and slowly pull on the lever – it will sink back to the bars if the seals are in poor condition. This can be easily confirmed, as a hard pull will make the lever firm again. Replacement is straightforward, but if you harbour any doubts about working on a safety critical item like the front brake, then a complete new replacement cylinder may be the better option. The sealing washers fitted to the union bolts compress easily, so unless they are perfect replace them.

03.59 Disc-equipped models have the master cylinder bolted to the headset. The fluid level is checked through the circular sight glass at the front.

HOW TO RESTORE CLASSIC LARGEFRAME VESPA SCOOTERS

03.60 Removal involves taking off the headset top as outlined previously, undoing the two socket-headed bolts that secure the cylinder, unplugging the brakelight switch wiring and undoing this brake pipe union.

03.61 The whole assembly can then be transferred to the bench for stripping.

03.62 The screws holding the reservoir cap are soft and go rusty, which is a very bad combination. If they won't budge use a drill bit slightly smaller than the head of the screw, and drill until you are below the lip of the lid, which can be removed along with the seal and plate under it.

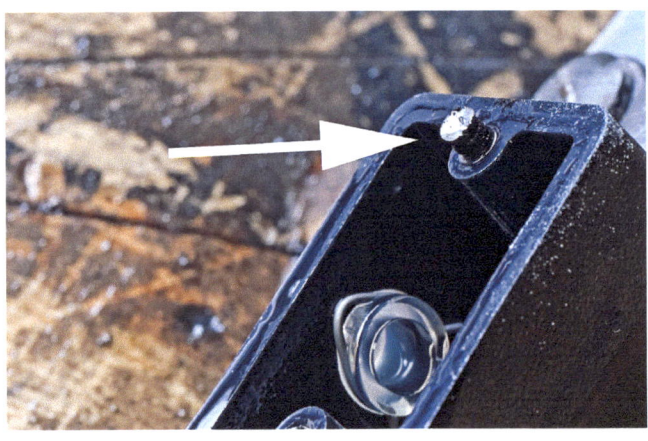

03.63 The remains of the lid screws (arrowed) can now be unwound. They are not usually that tight once you get a grip on them.

03.64 The brake lever pivot screw also suffers from corrosion, and can need some assistance from a set of grips to get it moving, as the screwdriver slot is again a bit soft and chews up easily.

03.65 This was from a very low mileage scooter, but the rust was well established on the pivot pin (arrowed) and washer.

03.66 The cylinder piston just pulls out of the body once the lever is removed.

FRONT END

03.67 There is a spring, two seals (white arrows – note the orientation of the left-hand one), and finally the outer dust seal bellows (yellow arrow). Do not bother trying to assess wear – replace the lot as a matter of course. The bits are very cheap.

03.68 The two seals can be prised free of the grooves using a slim pick. Once moving, they can be manipulated fairly easily.

03.69 With the piston stripped make sure that there are no burrs where the seals sit before replacing them.

03.70 The master cylinder parts come as a kit. Pattern versions are not much cheaper than genuine Piaggio ones.

03.71 Leave the seals soaking in fresh fluid for a couple of minutes before fitting.

03.72 The large dust seal can be fitted from the lever end, the other two from the chamber end. The round seal can be rolled into place, the chamfered one needs pulling, the brake fluid from the soaking acts as a lubricant to aid the process.

03.73 The rebuilt piston simply slides back into the chamber held in place by the lever. It is a little fiddly getting the pivot pin back in as you are working against spring pressure, but it's not too bad. A nyloc nut locks the pin in place once you have screwed it down. Make sure the lever is free to move – it is possible to over-tighten the pin.

HOW TO RESTORE CLASSIC LARGEFRAME VESPA SCOOTERS

03.74 The lid seal (bottom) pushes into the nylon pressing (middle), which then sits inside the lid (top).

03.75 New stainless steel lid screws are a good idea. They are stronger and obviously more corrosion resistant than the originals.

T5 MARK 1 HEADSET

The T5 Mark 1 has a rectangular headlight and a comprehensively equipped instrument panel with a rev counter, which can be analogue or digital. The main section is made from pressed steel rather than the alloy used on other Vespas. Disassembly is similar to the EFL PX once the covers are off (see exploded diagram). The headset is attached to the forks by a securing ring, which requires a pegged tool to undo it.

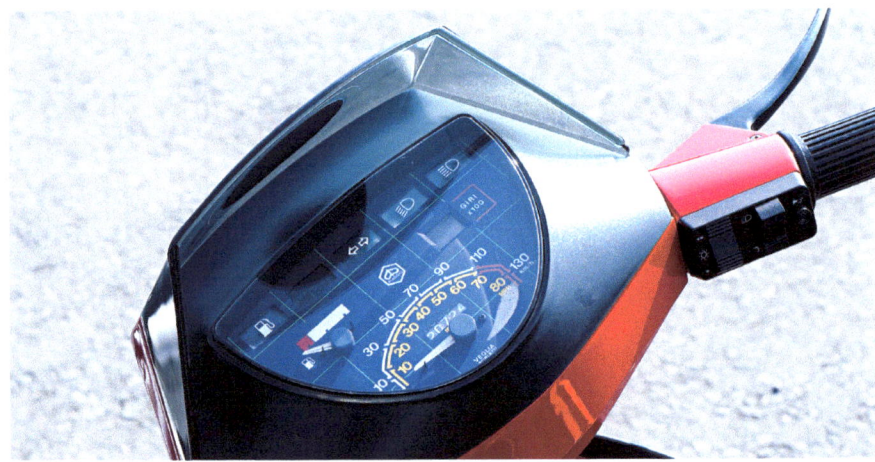

03.76 MkI T5s have a comprehensively equipped instrument panel including a rev counter (originally analogue then changed to digital).

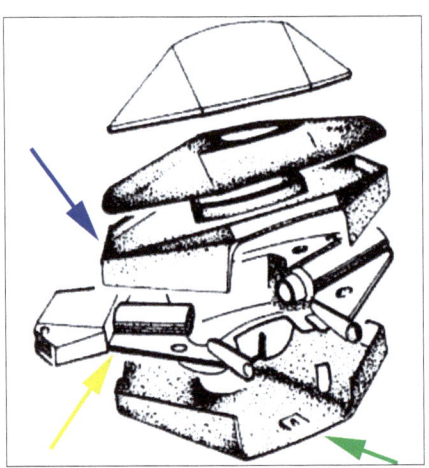

03.77 The gear and throttle tubes are held in a steel pressing (yellow arrow). The lower cover (green arrow) is plastic, the top (blue arrow) contains the instruments, and it lifts away just like the EFL version described above, with similar electrical connectors.

FORK STRIP/OVERHAUL (PRE-PX)

03.78 This is a Sprint front fork/hub assembly. It's very similar to the Rally, Super, etc, and remained in production until the introduction of the P series which is covered in a later section.

03.79 There are some small differences to the VBB type, and these will be indicated as we proceed.

FRONT END

03.80 To get the front mudguard off, the lower bearing race must be removed. It has a dust cover underneath, and both are an interference fit on an alloy casting on the fork.

03.81 Access to the bearing race will be improved with the mudguard loose, as a chisel or drift can then be inserted through the centre hole to act squarely on the seal holder. The top two bolts need to be removed, although in this case one was corroded into the alloy and required drilling out. Stainless steel replacements are available to prevent this happening again.

03.82 Under the mudguard more nuts will be visible. The corresponding bolt heads are under the alloy side trim where fitted, so this should be removed too, which usually involves removing a couple of 7mm nuts (one arrowed).

03.83 The trim bolts are square-headed and slide along inside the curved edges of the alloy. They can be removed completely for cleaning or replacement by sliding along to the end of the trim that's open.

03.84 The mudguard bolt heads are then accessible, and can be gripped to free the nuts under the guard.

03.85 The edge of the dust seal can be seen overlapping the alloy casting, but there isn't a lot to get at, so some care is needed when using a drift.

03.86 It will take a couple of sharp taps to get the race moving. Work around the edge as best you can, keeping it all square as it moves. Take care at this stage not to gouge the alloy under the seal – if you do, the damage will need dressing out afterwards. Once it has started moving it should become progressively easy. Once clear of the alloy casting it will be completely loose, and can be removed by hand.

03.87 The mudguard can now be removed. At first it doesn't look like it will come off, as casting protrusions on the fork appear larger than the hole in the guard, but by tilting and turning, the edge of the hole can be worked around these, and the guard lifted off.

HOW TO RESTORE CLASSIC LARGEFRAME VESPA SCOOTERS

03.88 The brake drum is held by a castellated nut secured by a split pin, so removal is straightforward when everything is in good condition. When faced with a rusty mess like this, do not waste your time trying to remove the pin – cut off the protruding ends, force a 22mm socket over the nut and undo. The remains of the pin can be drilled or pulled from the spindle once everything has been disassembled. The drum may require tapping around the edge to release it, but be careful – it is fragile.

03.89 If the scooter has been standing for some time, expect the drum to have corroded braking surfaces. In theory this can be skimmed, but there isn't a lot of material to play with, so if the rust has penetrated deeply then replacement is the only answer. Fortunately, replacements are currently available for virtually all models covered by this manual.

03.90 The shoes will almost certainly contain asbestos on old, unrestored scooters, so wash the whole assembly in brake cleaner before going any further, and avoid breathing in any dust.

03.91 Four stud hubs as fitted to the VBB will look like this once the drum, which is held in place by two screws, is removed.

03.92 Both shoes pivot on the same pin and are secured by a horseshoe clip, which is removed by spreading the ends and lifting away. The clips can be springy, and could fly off across the workshop.

03.93 Some early shoes overlap in this style at the pivot point, and obviously need to be released together, but the method is basically the same.

03.94 Twist the operating lever to spread the shoes on the brake cam and lift the top one upwards. Some corrosion may be present on the pivot pin, so spray with aerosol lubricant to ease progress. Use a screwdriver to help lift the shoe away from the backplate. The return spring is strong, so watch where you place your fingers during this process. Once the top shoe is off the other will lift away quite easily.

FRONT END

03.95 Before stripping the rest of the hub assembly, it is best to take out the speedo drive, because if you forget and drive out the axle it will damage the plastic gear wheel inside. Make a note of the cable run too, so the new parts can go back correctly. The knurled nut (arrowed) may need gentle persuasion to get it started, so use a pair of pliers, but be careful – it is easy to squash it if you are heavy-handed. There is a grease nipple on a separate ring immediately behind the nut, then the drive assembly, which should pull straight out.

03.96 Bend flat the tabs holding the link cover, then tap them off as they tend to stick. Underneath you will be faced with this.

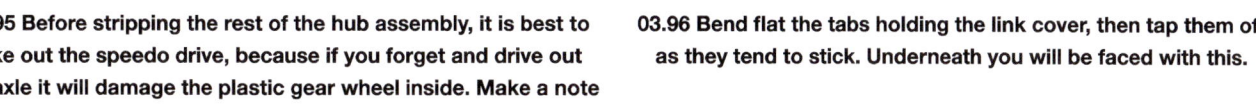

03.98 Undo the bolt holding the retaining plate between the two studs, and carefully tap the plate free of the grooves.

03.97 Remove the shock absorber bolts top and bottom, then pivot the shock absorber free. Test it for damping and check for leaks. Replacements are cheap.

03.99 One of the studs goes through the trunnion that holds the bottom of the suspension spring, and into the drum, where it acts as the pivot point for the shoes. This pin needs to be drifted out from the drum side. The picture shows it being tapped from the other side because the pin may well be reluctant to move freely, so apply a releasing agent and work it backwards and forwards until it will drift all the way out.

HOW TO RESTORE CLASSIC LARGEFRAME VESPA SCOOTERS

03.100 Undo the suspension spring top cap nut, and lever the cap away from the fork plate. The whole assembly should come free.

03.101 The bottom spring trunnion can then be pulled off the spring. This should have needle bearings in the centre with end caps. In this instance, it has all been badly damaged by corrosion, and replacement is the only answer. Check the pivot pins as well for signs of excess wear when confronted by damage like this.

03.102 The second pin acts as the pivot to the main fork leg. In this case the head was obscured by the brake backplate, in many cases there is a cutout, but where it is missing the plate has to be removed, which involves grinding away these small sections where the alloy of the hub has been peened over to secure it. Once ground away the plate just taps off. The pin is driven through from the drum side to release the hub from the fork. The inside of the fork should have needle rollers and a distance piece – once again, on this scooter they had almost completely disappeared due to corrosion and the pounding from continued use.

03.103 This hub washer is loose and locates in its own hole. Remove, clean and keep safe until reassembly.

03.104 The next job is to remove the axle and the bearings it runs on. There is a large cap (22mm nut size) that has to be undone first ...

03.105 ... which reveals a second 22mm nut. If you are using an impact wrench it should undo. If you are using a socket and ratchet, slide the drum back onto the axle and hold that whilst undoing this nut.

03.106 The VBB system is similar to the Sprint outlined so far, but relies on threaded pivots with securing nuts rather than pins, as can be seen. Disassembly, though, is virtually the same.

FRONT END

03.107 The axle now taps out through the hub from the side that had the 22mm nut. There is a machined recess to fit a drift into to aid removal.

03.108 If you have a VBB or similar with the four stud hub the removal process is the same, but the axle comes out like this with the flange attached.

03.109 There is a seal covering the axle bearing on the drum side. Lever this out.

03.110 The bearing is then revealed held in place by a circlip (arrowed), which should be removed.

03.111 Both bearings can be drifted out – the fork link side with a slim drift first, then the drum side where a larger drift can be used.

03.112 The bearings should automatically be replaced.

03.113 The forks now only have the internal pin bearings and caps left to remove. These caps have to be driven out from the inside of the tube. They are often tight.

03.114 Once the caps (yellow arrows) are off, the needle roller bearings (white arrows) can be driven out. This is done from the inside of the tube out, and is a little awkward as there is not much of an edge to get a drift on, but the washers (blue arrows) act as an extra lip until they deform under the bashing. There is also a spacer sleeve (green arrow) that can be drifted out if you have a replacement ready to fit. It doesn't come with most pivot pin sets, but it is still a good idea to take out the old one even if it will be refitted, in order to properly clean out the fork tube.

HOW TO RESTORE CLASSIC LARGEFRAME VESPA SCOOTERS

03.115 The parts for the rebuild were sourced as a kit in this instance, although on reflection it might have been better just to replace the necessary parts and keep as much as possible of the original setup.

03.116 The supplied hub had damage and was the wrong colour, so a repaint was in order. The surface was flattened in preparation for the new top coat.

03.117 A light dusting with wheel silver smartened it up again, and made it look more original.

03.118 The forks were treated to a clean-up next. The threads for the column bearing nuts were de-rusted, then the bottom cleaned off with a wire brush on a grinder, before receiving a coat of wheel silver just like the hub.

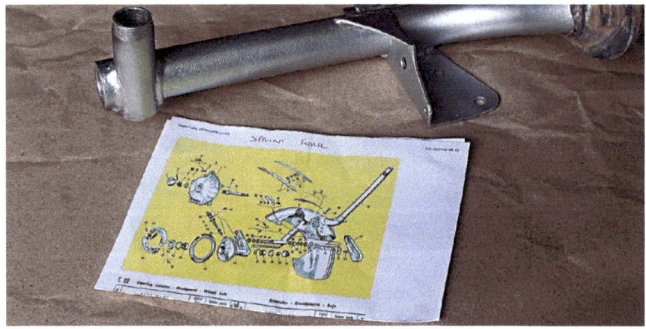

03.119 A copy of the relevant page from a parts manual is handy to have nearby when you are dealing with an assembly with lots of parts. Tape it to your work table for quick reference.

03.120 The first job is to fit the main pivot bearing set.

FRONT END

03.121 Grease the tube where it is all going to go first.

03.122 Tap in the central sleeve (if you removed it to begin with) with the slot in line with the hole for the grease nipple.

03.123 Put a washer in the tube next and tap down into place.

03.124 The bearings follow. They are needle rollers, so find a drift that fits as closely as possible to the outer diameter. Grease them well before inserting. If they have a number stamped in the outer edge, apply force from that side when fitting.

03.125 Once down, put in the second washer followed by the end cap. The other side is a repeat of this process.

03.126 Pack the larger of the two wheel bearings with grease, as it is going in first.

03.127 Use a drift to seat the bearing. This one was a tight fit, so once again a well-fitting drift is essential. When seated correctly the hammer note will change to a ring rather than a thud. The groove for the circlip should be clearly visible and the clip can be inserted. The second bearing is tapped into the hub from the rear, again using a suitable drift ...

03.128 ... followed by the oil seal, which can be seated with thumb pressure alone.

HOW TO RESTORE CLASSIC LARGEFRAME VESPA SCOOTERS

03.129 The hub is ready to go on the forks, so start by tapping the locating pin through the main pivot, ensuring that the cutout at the end will be in the correct place for its locating plate. Use a soft-faced hammer particularly with a new pin as they are often softer than the original Vespa part.

03.130 Don't forget to put the cleaned washer from earlier back into its locating hole before assembling the hub and finally driving the pin home.

03.131 The new spring pivot had a bush rather than rollers, cheaper to manufacture no doubt, and possibly more robust if kept well greased.

03.132 The bottom spring pivot can go on next after lubricating it and attaching the spring seat, having made sure it is the correct way up. Don't forget the spacer washers, and check that parts diagram to make sure it is all in the right place. Now that both pins are back, refit the securing plate and tighten the securing bolt.

03.133 The axle can be fitted next. Remember to fit the small spacer (arrowed) on the shaft. It's a tight fit, so use a deep socket of the right diameter as a drift and a couple of gentle taps will get it moving.

03.134 Grease the shaft well before fitting.

03.135 It should push in by hand until this point, where it is just about to enter the bearing races.

FRONT END

03.136 Fit the hub nut back to front, and slightly proud of the shaft, to protect the threads and split pin hole, then tap the shaft through with a soft hammer.

03.137 Fit the woodruff key and make sure that it fits properly in the machined slot.

03.138 Fit the large spacer then the securing nut (you may have to refit the brake drum for a moment to stop the axle spinning as you do up the nut).

03.139 Finish off by fitting the screwed dust cap.

03.140 Put a little copper grease on the brake pivot and slide it through the backplate.

03.141 The kit came with new shoes but the compound was suspiciously soft when the edge was chamfered before fitting. If the drum backplate was removed to get the pin out, replace it now.

87

03.142 The metal shoe plates need to be secured. A pair of side-cutters will bend over the tabs enough to hold them.

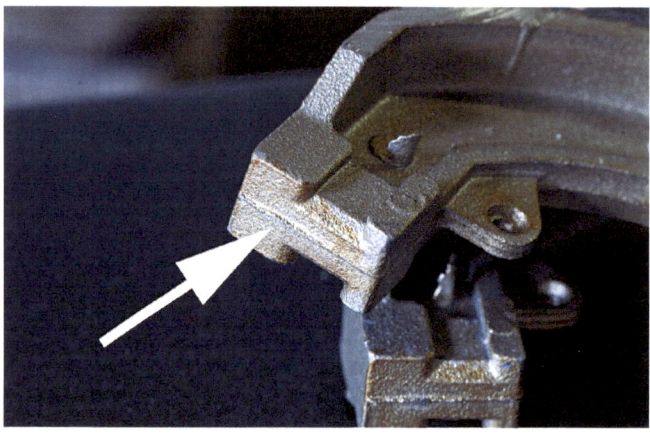

03.143 When the new drum was slipped in place it was very tight. The shoes were checked, and this moulding flash had to be sanded off. The shoes also had a high spot.

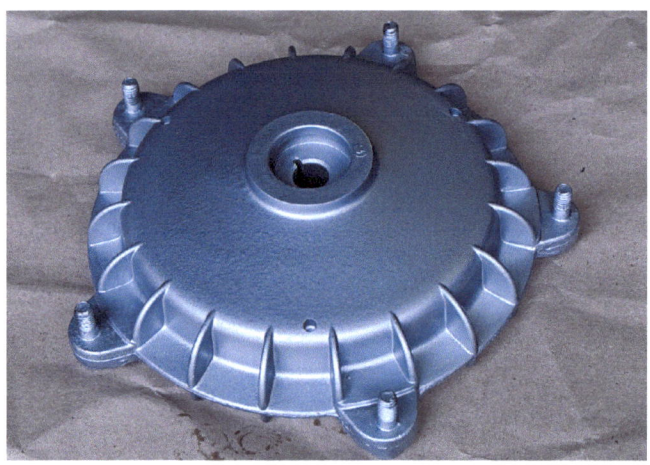

03.144 New drums are available for most models, although the quality can vary.

03.145 The high spot on the shoes was dealt with initially by some careful sanding with 80 production paper, which removed the offending hump.

03.146 Grooved shoes or ones with an upgraded compound can be used to improve stopping power. They also tend to be better made and fit better.

03.147 The brake woes, unfortunately, did not end there. The adjuster sleeve and locknut supplied in the kit were far too large. The old one was salvaged, sanded down, and sprayed with silver paint.

FRONT END

03.148 The lower spring mount should be tightened fully, ready for the spring installation.

03.149 When ordering a new spring make sure the length is correct – measure the old one before placing your order as there are a few variations. This spring was roughly finished with a poor cut at the end and very thin chrome on the inside of the spiral. The end was cleaned up using an air cut-off tool. Once in use it quickly became apparent that it was even soggier than the worn-out original and hit the hub casting on full compression, which was dangerous.

03.150 This is one of Stoffi's (an Austrian scooter shop) uprated springs, they are 33 per cent firmer than standard, which helps cut front end dive, and are clearly better finished than the cheaper options.

03.151 The top cup has to be attached next. This one was mis-pressed – the centre raised section wasn't circular so wouldn't go on the spring initially. Some careful tapping with a punch got the shape somewhere right.

03.152 With the bottom of the spring screwed on the lower cup, the top has to be levered with a large screwdriver or similar until it is trapped under the fork plate. Once like this it can be gently tapped until the threaded section pops through the hole in the plate. This process is obviously tougher if an uprated spring has been selected.

03.153 The shock absorber just bolts on with two small lugs to aid location at the bottom. The fork needs to be compressed, which is fairly easy to do, but an assistant to slide the bolts in is helpful. The drum is resting on a cardboard box to stop it getting scratched on the workshop floor.

03.154 Old and new speedo drives. Although they look very similar, the new one supplied in the kit wouldn't fit the hub included in the same box.

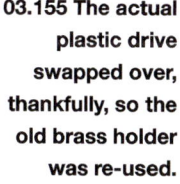

03.155 The actual plastic drive swapped over, thankfully, so the old brass holder was re-used.

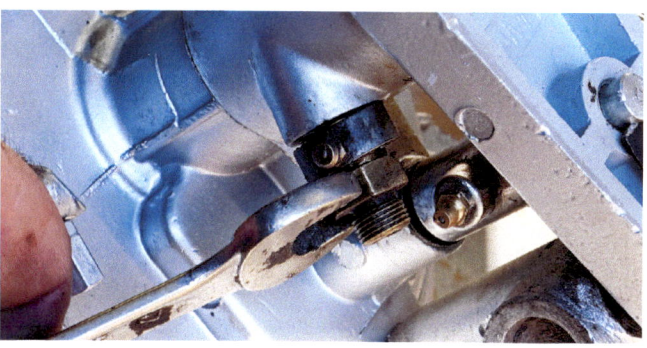

89

HOW TO RESTORE CLASSIC LARGEFRAME VESPA SCOOTERS

03.156 A new link cover was bought in alloy. It simply pushes over the casting, with the small locating tabs being bent over to secure it.

03.157 If a new mudguard is being used, it may not come with side-mounting holes drilled. If that is the case, secure the top mounts, then use a scriber to mark where the new holes will need to be drilled.

03.158 A hole cutter was used in this case from the outside, after a pilot hole had been made from the markings made on the inside.

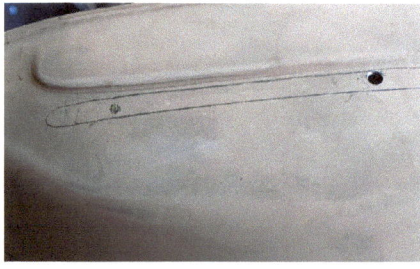

03.159 If you intend to reinstate the trim, mark its position on the guard using your main mounting holes as reference then mark the position of the smaller ones and drill to suit.

03.160 The last job is to run the cables through the forks ready for refitting. The speedo cable end will need stripping first. The plastic ferrule on the left just pulls off, followed by the knurled ring and plastic cover.

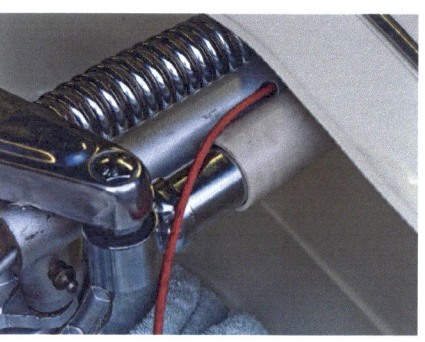

03.161 To get the cable down through the forks, a guide wire can be pushed through and the new one taped to it. This may be awkward, as the cable wants to stick at the bend of the forks.

03.162 It may be easier to push the new outer cable down from the top of the forks watching for its arrival at the outlet hole. Once the end becomes visible, a small screwdriver can be used to direct the cable out through the hole. The inner is then threaded through and the ferrule, ring and cover refitted.

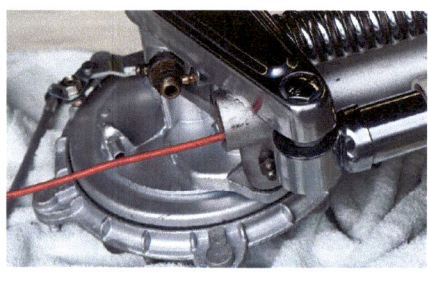

03.163 The front brake cable goes straight through the fork and out of the bottom. The guide system can be used, although the new cable will probably push down and through on its own without any other assistance.

03.164 These are the forks pictured at the start of this section, but now fully refurbished and ready for many more miles of use.

FRONT END

FORK STRIP/OVERHAUL PX

03.166 Disc brake forks share many of the components of their earlier drum incarnation.

03.165 A well-used PX front fork and hub. Obviously rusty and missing its link cover, it also suffered from non-existent damping and a wobbly pivot.

03.167 The mudguard is held by three bolts on top and another on the side. It can be removed from the forks without taking off the lower bearing race – an improvement on earlier scooters.

03.168 The shock absorber is removed by first undoing two nuts at the top. The corresponding bolt heads are held captive by the alloy casting.

03.169 At the bottom is another pair of nuts to undo. This time the bolt heads need to be held to loosen these. On disc models these nuts are part of the shock body, so the bolts alone need to be undone to release them.

HOW TO RESTORE CLASSIC LARGEFRAME VESPA SCOOTERS

03.170 The shock has a top mounting plate, which can be undone for cleaning and replacement of the two rubber isolating bushes. The shaft of the shock has a screw slot to hold it whilst the nut is undone.

03.171 The shock absorber can be dismantled for cleaning by undoing the top cap (arrowed). The spring can be replaced or uprated, but the main body is sealed so will have to be replaced if defective or leaking. A complete new assembly is the most usual course of action.

03.172 The speedo cable is held in place by a plate (arrowed). It is removed by undoing the bolt.

03.173 The whole assembly will probably pull out as one. It comprises rubber bung (yellow arrow), bush (white arrow), and plastic speedo drive (blue arrow).

03.174 Disc or drum, the hub is secured by a split pin through a locking cage, under which is a nut. Once these are removed the drum or disc carrier should pull off, although a gentle tap from behind with a soft-faced hammer may be useful.

03.175 With the hub off, a circlip should be visible in the depths. It may be covered in grease, so wipe the area clear.

03.176 The disc setup will look like this.

03.177 It has exactly the same circlip inside the recess under the grease.

FRONT END

03.178 With the circlip removed pull the hub carrier/backplate off the spindle. There will be rubber seals under it (arrowed) although they may have broken up or be stuck to the hub, so don't worry about them at the moment.

03.179 With the backplate on a bench, lever out the large seal.

03.180 There should be a loose washer in there too (arrowed), which will probably be stuck in the old grease. The two backplate bearings will be clearly visible.

03.181 Use a slim drift as there isn't a lot to rest the end on, and drive the bearings out of the backplate from the inside. This side is easy as there is room underneath for the bearing to drop into.

03.182 To get the other one out the backplate will need supporting to provide a suitable void for the bearing to drop into; a large socket does the trick.

03.183 The bearings are the same in the disc hub carrier, and are removed in the same way.

93

HOW TO RESTORE CLASSIC LARGEFRAME VESPA SCOOTERS

03.184 Strip and degrease the backplate. Shoe removal is the same as outlined previously in the Sprint section, although the PX has two pivot posts. A coat of paint leaves it ready for reassembly.

03.185 There are two wheel bearings in the drum/disc carrier, the first is held by a circlip that has to be removed (arrowed).

03.186 The bearing is drifted out from the inside.

03.187 The other bearing has a seal on top, which has to be levered out.

03.188 The bearing can then be knocked out like the other side.

03.189 The drum can then be degreased, sanded and painted.

03.190 Everything needed for the overhaul can be bought as a kit or as individual components. The kit is cheaper.

FRONT END

03.191 The backplate bearings are small and delicate. Always apply pressure to the side with the markings stamped in.

03.192 Use a close-fitting socket as a drift (dedicated tools are available for this job if you want to use them), and seat the bearings.

03.193 Grease them well.

03.194 Refit the large seal and grease its lip.

03.195 The bearings in the drum can then be inserted. Again, use a close-fitting socket on the outside of the bearing race.

03.196 Refit the circlip.

03.197 Insert the bearing on the other side of the drum.

HOW TO RESTORE CLASSIC LARGEFRAME VESPA SCOOTERS

03.198 Followed by the new seal which should sit flush with the surface.

03.199 The seals on this link pin are shot, which allowed water and road debris to get into the joint and wear the pin and bearings.

03.200 The pin bearings are covered by these washers, which may be attached or loose depending on whether or not they are original.

03.201 Warm the alloy of the pivot and the steel of the fork.

03.202 Using a drift, hammer out the pin, which will probably take the bearings with it. This is hard going, and may need a further application of heat around the fork end to achieve. If you cannot get it going ask a local engineering shop to press out the pin.

03.203 Clean the fork, de-rust, and paint as required before beginning reassembly.

FRONT END

03.204 Fit the brake and speedo cables using the techniques outlined earlier in the Sprint section.

03.205 A new pivot pin should come complete with seals.

03.206 The first bush can be pressed in using a socket resting on the inner face of the washer, not the petals. They go in a lot easier than they come out.

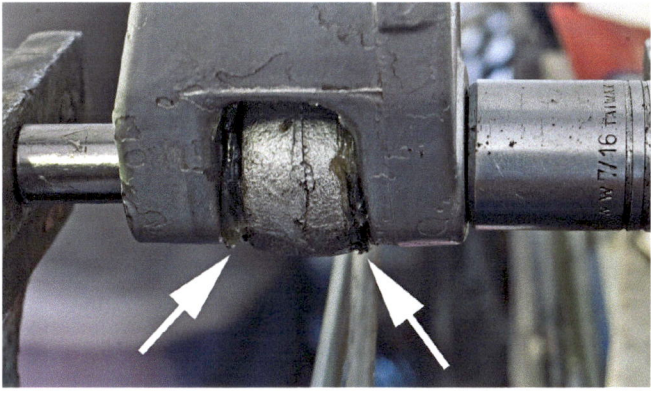

03.207 The pin can then be pressed in. The socket is acting on the outside of the bearing already fitted to stop it being pushed out in the process. The large O ring seals (arrowed) were a very poor fit and would not stay in place when the fork was offered up. One way round this is to use a little superglue and stick them to the fork in a couple of places to hold them in position.

03.208 The second bearing can then be fitted over the pin. Finish the job by tapping the outer edges of the petals down with a socket. An alternative method for the whole job is to insert the pin without either bearing in place, and then fit them both around the pin. Both systems were tried and both work.

03.209 The large round rubber O ring and the metal shim slide in place and the pin can then be greased.

03.210 Another rubber O ring sits inside the backplate.

HOW TO RESTORE CLASSIC LARGEFRAME VESPA SCOOTERS

03.211 The backplate can then be placed over the pin.

03.212 A washer with a cutout goes on next.

03.213 The cutout matches a section on the pin, note the groove as well. This is where the circlip will fit.

03.214 The circlip is expanded, slipped down the shaft and snapped into place.

03.215 The shock absorber can be refitted with new mounting rubbers.

03.216 Once the bottom mount is on, the backplate is secured to the forks once more. This one is missing its captive nut (disc model). A loose one will do just as well.

03.217 With the backplate secure, new brake shoes can be fitted.

03.218 The drum or disc carrier can now be refitted.

FRONT END

03.219 The speedo drive should be greased and the bush cleaned then inserted.

03.220 The speedo cable can be reattached. Access is a little awkward, but easier than when the forks are on the scooter.

03.221 A new link cover can be fitted – they are plastic on the PX and cheap. Decorative versions can be bought.

03.222 The same forks as at the beginning of the sequence, but now fully overhauled ready for use.

BRAKE CALIPER

The most likely problems are leaking seals and sticking caliper pistons. The main components are robust and of good quality, and only let down by the fittings, which are prone to corrosion that can seriously hamper disassembly. Once again, wholesale replacement may be the better option in many cases.

The caliper pistons are best removed by pumping them out whilst the hydraulics are still attached. If the line has already been split then compressed air will do the same job. If air is not available, weld a grease nipple to a suitable brake line nut and insert it into the bleed nipple hole, then pump the caliper piston cavity full of grease. This will force the piston out.

03.223 The caliper should have a plastic cover over the pads, but it is often missing. If it is there, it simply pulls off.

03.224 Exposing the pads and their securing pin.

03.225 The pin is held by this small clip – grip it with pliers and pull free. Replace it if it's this corroded.

03.226 The pin is then drifted through from the clip side. It is often corroded and sticks. If so, lubricate and work it backwards and forwards until free.

03.227 Remove the anti-rattle plate, then the pads lift up and out of the caliper.

HOW TO RESTORE CLASSIC LARGEFRAME VESPA SCOOTERS

03.228 If the hydraulics are still attached, pump the pistons out. Here the pads are arrowed.

03.229 The hydraulic line is held by this banjo bolt. Take note of the washers fitted.

03.230 Inspect the washers for signs of crushing. Replace if necessary.

03.231 The caliper body can be removed by undoing these bolts. The bolts shown above hold the caliper halves together.

03.232 The bolts holding together the caliper halves suffer badly from corrosion, and in this case only one of the four came undone – one snapped (pictured), and the other two rounded their heads off.

03.233 To remove bolts with rounded heads, take a drill bit slightly larger than the socket recess of the head, and drill until it separates from the shaft of the bolt as pictured.

03.237 With the heads off, the caliper can be split. The amount of corrosion on the bolt shafts is incredible but not uncommon.

FRONT END

03.234 Self-locking pliers may get enough grip to unscrew the remains of the bolts.

03.235 If not, drill down the centre of the bolt and use an extractor. The bolts can be incredibly stubborn even when reduced to a thin shell as here.

03.236 The pistons do not seem to suffer badly. Check them for marking or corrosion which might damage the seals.

03.237 The seals sit in the caliper halves and can be removed with a sharp pick or thin screwdriver. Check the grooves they sit in (arrowed) for damage.

03.238 New seals look too large, but just need compressing to get them into the opening. They expand once in their groove. Lubricate them with brake fluid before fitting. They are symmetrical, so you don't need to worry about orientation.

03.239 There is a further small seal between the caliper halves, which sits in this recess.

HOW TO RESTORE CLASSIC LARGEFRAME VESPA SCOOTERS

03.240 Use copper grease on all the bolts when reassembling.

03.241 Apply a small amount to the backs of the brake pads, too.

03.242 The anti-rattle clip has an arrow to indicate fitting direction; it points upward.

03.243 The rebuilt caliper ready to refit.

STEERING HEAD BEARINGS (ALL)

With the exception of some very early models in the last year of the fifties (and Spanish Motovespas as late as the mid-sixties), all models use the same caged bearings and tracks, which makes part ordering very easy. Loose ball models are also catered for, although stockists are fewer. A conversion kit to update to the caged setup is also on the market.

03.249 With the headset removed, the top of the steering column is exposed. Even if it is rusty like this, two notched rings sandwiching a plate should be clearly visible with the ball bearings underneath them.

FRONT END

03.244 The top ring will be tight, or should be. There are C spanners available for this job (see later), but when the components are this bad a drift can be used to get the ring moving, as it will be replaced anyway.

03.245 Unscrew the top ring completely, lubricating it as necessary to aid removal.

03.246 The middle plate should just pull free.

03.247 Undo the bottom ring and the forks are ready to pull free of the frame. If you have a scooter from the very early '60s, the ball bearings will be loose. Most scooters covered by this book have caged balls, which are obviously much easier to handle.

03.248 With the forks off, the races in the frame need removing. Once again, there are special tools available, but a long drift like this is all you really need.

03.249 Slide the drift into the frame from the bottom first, and locate the end on the shoulder of the race (arrowed). There isn't a lot to grip, so be careful.

HOW TO RESTORE CLASSIC LARGEFRAME VESPA SCOOTERS

03.250 A couple of sharp taps should see it free of the frame.

03.251 Examine the race for wear – this one is appalling, and even minor signs of scuffing or blueing should be enough to condemn the race and bearing, as replacements are readily available and very cheap.

03.252 The bottom race is harder to deal with, as the lip is obscured by the frame pressing. If you place an investigative finger behind the race you will feel a small gap – this is used to get the race out. A leg from a puller set slipped behind the lip with a chisel or similar to jam it in place is fine. Use the drift against the leg through the frame as before. It can feel like you need three hands to manage this, but it is possible on your own.

03.253 Here you can see the puller leg type you need to use, and the old race it successfully removed.

03.254 With the race out of the way, you can see how the inner tube in the frame prevents a straight hit on the race.

03.255 The design of the steering head bearings is similar throughout the Vespa range, which has kept prices remarkably low. This type uses loose balls, which were only fitted at the very beginning of the rotary era, but lingered into the mid-'60s on Motovespas.

FRONT END

03.256 Caged bearings like these are far more common, and a lot easier to work with.

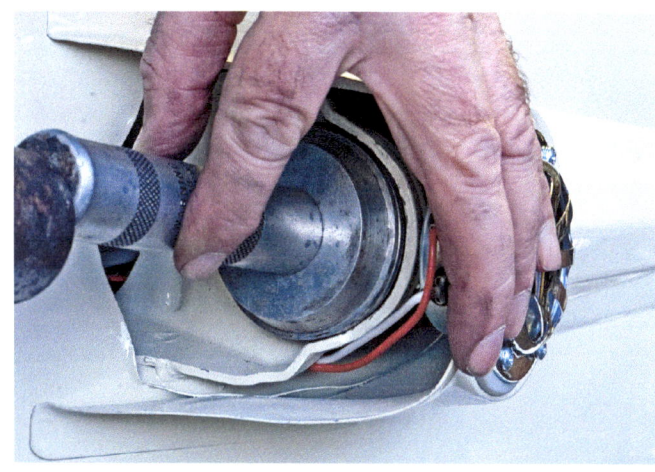

03.257 The bottom race is the hardest to get into place. When fitting you can only use the outer lip to apply force – never allow anything to hit the track, or it will be ruined. Clean any paint from the inside of the frame seat, then use a bearing driver to knock the race into place. It can be tough and need a fair bit of tapping. Make sure that it is fully home and square.

03.258 The dust seal and bottom inner race can be tapped into place using a slim drift on the inner edge of the race, away from the track. Work your way around the edge bit by bit and it will drop into position relatively easily. These are loose balls which need to be 'glued' to the race with grease before lifting the fork into place. The caged type just drop into place, but also need greasing well before the fork is put back.

03.259 The top outer race (bottom arrow) taps into the frame easily. Loose bearings are a real pain up top, as there is a tendency for them to slide down under their own weight and out of the bearing track, not helped by the fact that the fork won't sit square until the securing rings are fitted. The inner race (second from bottom arrow) is tightened. This has to be tight, yet loose enough that the forks turn freely throughout their complete arc without any tight spots. Next comes the flat washer (second arrow from top), followed by the top ring (not surprisingly, the top arrow).

03.260 The use of a drift was fine for removing the old bearing rings, but will damage new ones, so C spanners are a must on reassembly. Unfortunately some are poorly made – this set came from a mail order firm, and the ends deformed after one job.

Chapter 4
Frame

PAINT REMOVAL/ASSESSMENT

The first consideration is whether your scooter's condition warrants removing all previous coatings and getting back to bare steel. If it has spent its life in a warm climate, then fading and surface rust may be all you have to contend with, and some simple sanding may be sufficient. If the rust looks like it has got a good grip then something more drastic may be required, and getting back to sound metal might be the only sensible option.

Dipping

This is an efficient but expensive process, especially if you opt to have the metal phosphate etched at the same time. One recent quote for a frame was 20 times the amount that was subsequently spent having it blasted at a local agricultural engineers. If you do choose to have your frame dipped, talk to the operator and ensure that they are happy with drainage – you don't want any additional holes being added without your knowledge.

Blasting

This can vary in severity depending on the choice of media and the skill and experience of the operator. It's a relatively cheap way of getting the frame back to bare metal, but make sure the firm you use has done scooters before or you could end up with wavy legshields. Blasting won't remove old underseal or heavily congealed oils, so the frame will have to be degreased, and as much of the contamination removed as possible before handing it over to your chosen blaster. If the chassis number is not well stamped make sure you point out the area to the operative, and ask them not to linger over it. The freshly blasted frame must be etch-coated or at the very least primed as quickly as possible, or rust will take hold again very quickly. Getting all the old blast media out of the central tunnel pressing can be time consuming, but is necessary before painting starts in earnest.

04.2 Pressings such as the horn cast are difficult to get into, and it doesn't get inside box sections either, as we shall see.

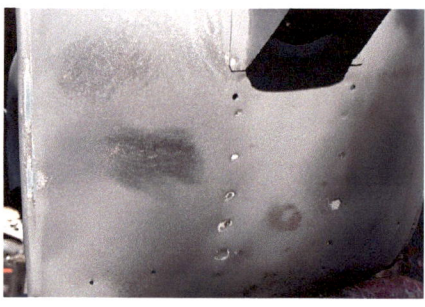

04.1 Blasting is quick, but not 100 per cent effective. Small pockets of paint may still be stuck in spot weld depressions, for example. There is also the danger that unsupported areas like the legshields may be distorted if the blast pressure is too high.

FRAME

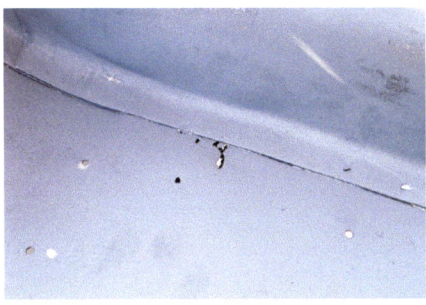

04.3 Examine the metal very closely. Some damage may be no bigger than a pin hole. Mark it if it is not immediately obvious – you don't want to miss anything when you wheel out the welder later.

04.4 Freshly blasted steel will start to rust even if kept inside, so a coat of etch primer is a good idea. This can be bought in aerosol form, as well as the traditional stuff for spray gun application.

04.5 Read any safety instructions carefully, as etch can be unpleasant stuff. As a minimum wear a mask.

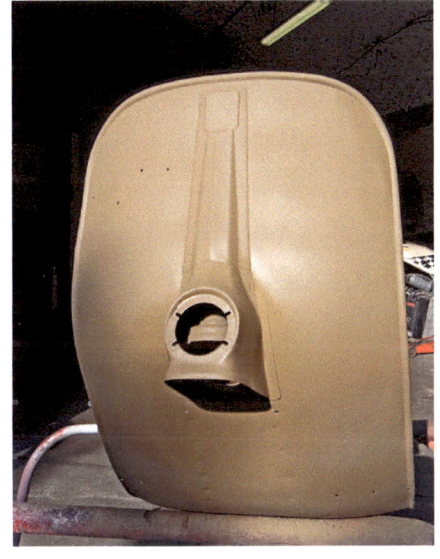

04.6 Once covered, the frame can be handled and stored without worrying about corrosion getting a grip again.

SODA BLASTING
A relative newcomer to the field, this technique appears to have the efficiency of traditional blasting without the potential for damage. Check for any conditions regarding over-painting before making your decision, and talk to the service provider about residue in the legshield and other panel seams.

PAINT STRIPPER
This is a slow and messy process, but ultimately effective. Modern formulations do not seem as powerful as they used to be, so it could prove an expensive option. Read the safety instructions on the tin carefully before use, cover up any bare skin and always wear eye protection.

ABRASIVES
The quickest way to get back to the metal at home is to use a twisted wire brush on an angle grinder, the flat versions being more useful than the cupped variety. This process is quite vicious, though, so once again use eye and hand protection and wear thick overalls, as bits of wire, rusty old frame and dust will be flying around. A dual action sander with a 40s disc will also do the job, but much more slowly. Either choice may also require some help from paint stripper to get into tight spots, and neither can get into seams fully.

04.7 If you intend to use abrasives, a knotted wire wheel on an angle grinder rips through old paint and rust very well. Wear eye protection though, as bits of wire tend to break off.

04.8 It can be a depressing job watching your scooter disappear as you work. Pitting like this will mean wholesale replacement of the old metal.

04.9 A dual action sander fitted with a 40 grade disc is pretty effective too, although it cannot reach into the edges very well.

107

HOW TO RESTORE CLASSIC LARGEFRAME VESPA SCOOTERS

WELDING

The following sections on frame repair assume that welding equipment is available, along with the skills to use it. Mig is the best process for home use, and the basics can be learnt very quickly. Have a look for a course at a local adult education centre – it is well worth learning. The cost of a DIY mig welder is reasonable compared to paying someone else to do extensive repairs, and it really is a useful skill to acquire.

Floor replacement

The photo sequence shows the floor being replaced from the underside of the scooter. This preserves the original spot welds on the upper face of the tunnel, so when the work is completed the scooter continues to look original and unmolested. If the rest of the frame is sound it probably isn't necessary to add a brace before removing the floor. If it isn't, or if you wish to err on the side of caution, then run a length of box section steel between the seat-nose mounting area and the frame just below the headstock. Tack welds are sufficient to hold it in place.

04.10 Replacement floor pressings can be bought for all rotary valve largeframes. This one is from Vietnam and was cheap. Italian-made versions that come ready shaped at the rear can be bought for around three times the price. Measure the new floor carefully from an area of the rear floorboard that is also accessible on the scooter.

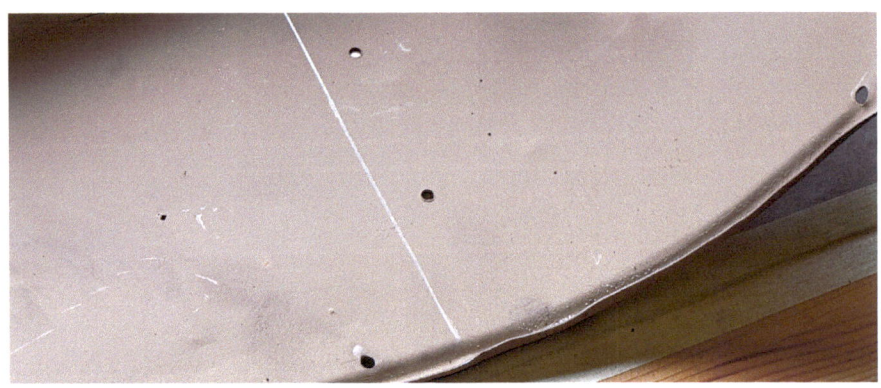

04.11 Transfer that measurement to the old floor, scribing a clear line. It is probably a good idea at this stage to make your line on the 'safe' side of the actual measurement, then trim later.

04.12 Make your cut with an angle grinder fitted with a plasma disc. These are around one third the thickness of a normal cutting disc and ideal for precise work. The downside is that as they are so thin they will not tolerate any side loading without shattering, so be careful.

04.13 The floorpan on each side of the tunnel has been cut off here. It is better to remove the old panel in chunks, as it reduces the weight acting on what is left and so reduces the risk of any distortion. The centre section under the tunnel is roughly marked out ready for cutting next.

FRAME

04.14 With it gone there remains only the strips spot welded to the underside of the central tunnel to get rid of. Find the welds and grind them down.

04.15 The strip can then be removed with a slim sharp bolster chisel. The weakened welds can clearly be seen (arrowed).

04.16 The folded remains of the floor at the back can now be dealt with.

04.17 An angle grinder can be used to weaken the spot welds, then the old sections chiselled off.

04.18 The inside of the tunnel may be rusty. If so, rub it down with some coarse paper. Apply a good rust killer to hold back future rusting.

04.19 Slide the new floor into place, and once lined up (and the old floor trimmed down at the front if you chose to cut on the safe side initially) mark the position of the tunnel and stand holes, so you can get it back in exactly the right place once it's drilled for the plug welds that will be used to hold it.

109

HOW TO RESTORE CLASSIC LARGEFRAME VESPA SCOOTERS

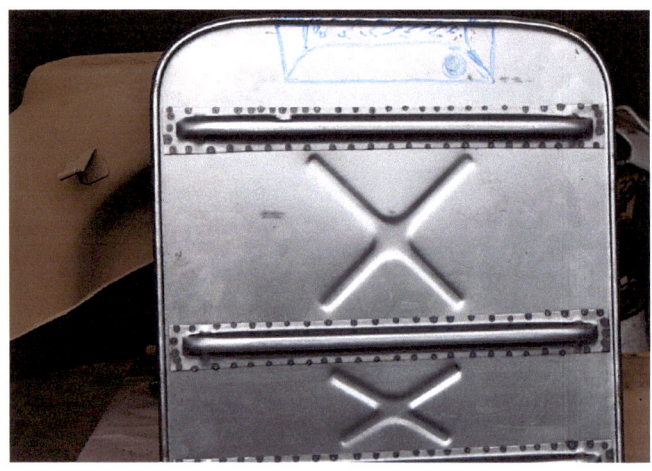

04.20 The new floor had some scribed lines marking the section that needed cutting out at the back. These are roughly indicated here with marker pen for the purposes of the photo.

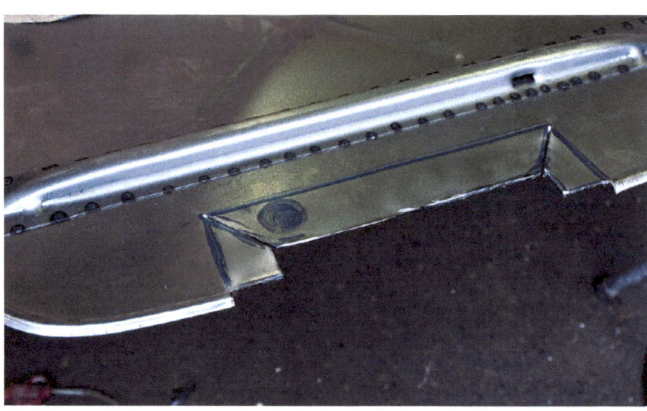

04.21 Initial cuts were made, including the lipped edge.

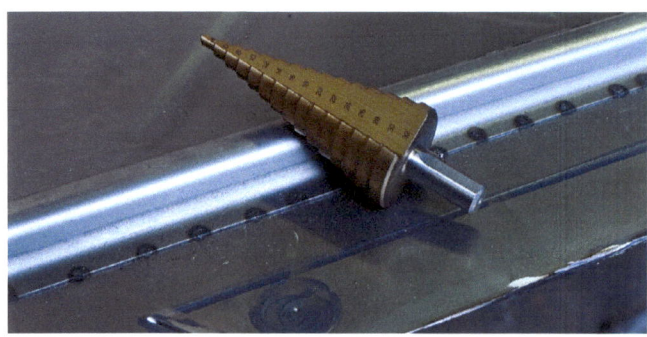

04.22 A hole cutter is useful for the cable hole. If you do not have one, drilling and filing will give the same result, just more slowly.

04.23 The inside of the tunnel was treated to a good coat of zinc-rich paint. Some of this will burn away during the welding, but most will survive to protect the steel for some time to come.

04.24 It is perfectly possible to replace a floor with all the cabling and electrics still in place. Use masking tape to attach it to the upper inside face of the tunnel, which will keep it away from the heat of welding. The masking tape will lose its grip within a short time, and the whole lot will drop back into place once the scooter is in use.

04.25 The new floor can be held at the edge with self-locking pliers, but these Intergrips are ideal for keeping it in place in the middle of the cut. They also hold the steel apart by just the right amount for a good penetrating weld.

FRAME

04.26 A couple of small welds on each side will hold the front whilst the rest of the pan is tacked in place. Double-check your alignment marks.

04.27 With the underside drilled and a couple of plug welds made at the front and rear, deep clamps can be used to hold the new section tight to the tunnel whilst the welds are made. Alternatively a hammer handle can be pressed down on the steel to close any gaps as the welding is done.

04.28 Plug welding is strong, and once ground down it is invisible.

04.29 Once the underside is secured go back to the front and run a series of short welds to seam the join. Move from side to side as you go to prevent heat build-up, which could cause distortion.

04.30 Make sure that the weld is strong across the join. Excess material can be ground down later.

04.31 At the back the flaps can be bent up once they have been drilled ready for plugging.

HOW TO RESTORE CLASSIC LARGEFRAME VESPA SCOOTERS

04.32 Once the welding is complete go round and grind everything flush.

Box sections
The box pressings under the floor are rot-prone, but simple to replace. Unfortunately it is rare that they have suffered alone, and there is normally damage underneath them that will require additional work.

04.33 Box sections under the floor are a common rust spot. Even ones that appeared sound initially often crumble when blasted.

04.34 Remove them by drilling out the old spot welds, or as described in the floor section grind the welds and chisel off the remains. A dedicated spot weld drill bit with a flat face is expensive but cuts through the old steel without damaging the floor below: well worth the investment.

04.35 A chisel is useful as the box may still be a little stuck even once the spot welds have been drilled.

04.36 One drawback of blasting is clearly visible now: the floor under the box is rusty and holed. If the box wasn't replaced this corrosion would have continued unseen.

04.37 An angle grinder will cut out the rotten steel but a smaller air cut-off tool is better if you have access to one.

FRAME

04.38 Take care where the section passes over the central tunnel. Expect to find more corrosion trapped between the layers of steel here.

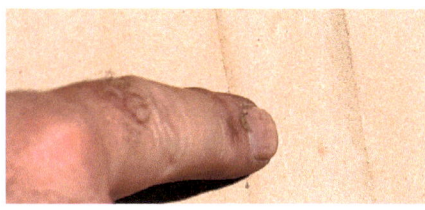

04.39 A replacement section of new steel will be required to fill the hole. As the edges are unlikely to be perfectly square unless you have a steady hand with a grinder, lay some thick paper over the hole and take a rubbing. A finger is shown here for the sake of the photo, but as the edge of the steel is sharp use a blunt instrument to make the necessary marks. Cut the paper and transfer the shape to your steel.

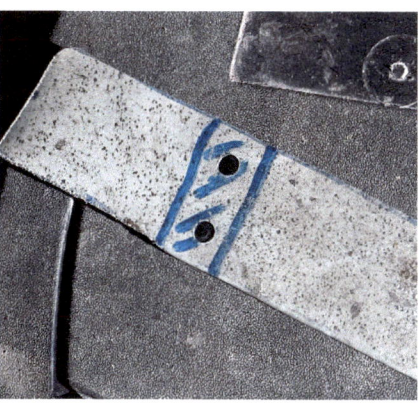

04.40 Once the new steel is cut, mark where it will pass over the tunnel and drill a couple of holes to plug weld through.

04.41 The edge of the cut hole may be slightly distorted from removing the rotten steel, so, using a block of wood as a support, work around the lip with a pry bar or similar tool and straighten it.

04.42 Intergrips can be used once again, or as shown here the magnetic head of an old pick-up tool to keep the steel in place ready for tacking.

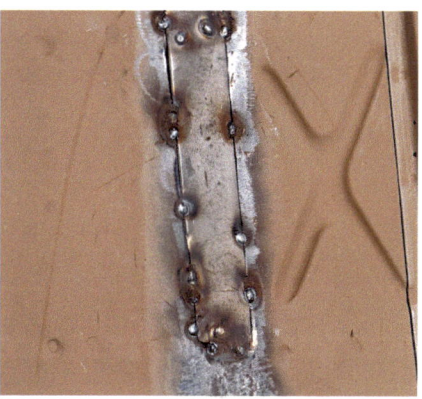

04.43 Make a few tacks around the edge and plug weld through to the tunnel.

04.44 Seam weld the plate, then grind flush.

04.45 New box sections in roughly the correct shape can be bought off the shelf. These had quite a lot of rust. The inside of the box should be painted before fitting.

HOW TO RESTORE CLASSIC LARGEFRAME VESPA SCOOTERS

Patch repair

It is possible that only a small section of your frame or floor may need repair and wholesale replacement isn't justified, or perhaps an area has rotted that has no repair section for sale. If that is the case, sectioning-in is a quick and straightforward solution.

04.46 Drill the new sections, clamp tightly to the floor, then plug weld. Grind the welds flush to finish.

04.47 This holing is where the legshields start to curve upwards behind the front wheel. It's a common place for rot.

04.48 A repair section was made and welded in using the same principles as the patch repair to the floor.

04.49 The repair will be invisible once ground flush and skimmed with a thin layer of filler.

Old holes/splits

These are the easiest body repairs of all, and ideal to start on if you are an inexperienced welder.

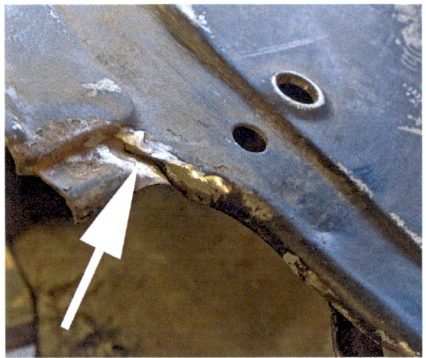

04.50 Small cracks around the rear end of the frame pressings are common.

04.51 Simply weld the seam and grind off.

114

FRAME

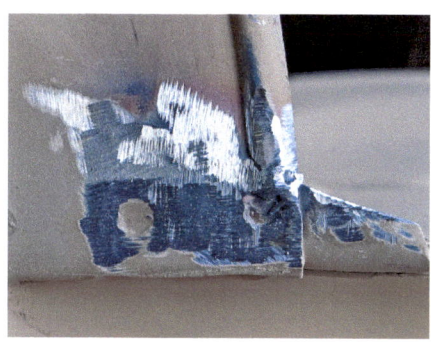

04.52 The back of the floor suffers in the same way. Once again, weld a seam then grind flush.

04.53 Elongation of the holes around the side panel mounts are also common, caused by the pin rattling against the frame as the panel seals wear.

04.54 Use a file until good solid metal is reached. Always square things off, if possible – it will make fabricating a repair section easier.

RUST KILLING

Having chopped out and replaced as much rusty metal as you can, there will still be some areas where corrosion lurks in the steel. There are dozens of rust neutralising formulations on the market and classic car magazines regularly run tests, so check online for any current recommendations. Always follow the manufacturers instructions for the best results and be liberal with the application making sure that it is brushed deeply into seams and panel gaps.

04.55 Weld in the new steel and finish off by running a drill through the hole to make sure it's neat.

04.56 Wherever welding has taken place treat the area with a good quality rust treatment as soon as possible, as it's the most likely spot for new rust to break out.

DENT REMOVAL

Panel beating is a skill that takes years to acquire, but there is no reason why a beginner should not have a go with their Vespa. Its single skin construction allows good access, and final imperfections can be lost with a skim of filler. Start the repair process by working back from the edge of any damage to the point of impact, working slowly – lots of small taps with a hammer rather than large belts. Support the other side of the metal whilst you work, either with a metal dolly, a block of wood, or simply by resting the panel on a workbench. Make use of anything that will help to check your progress – for example, hold up lamps, indicator mounts, or trim to the steel and see if your new contour matches up. Try out the techniques on a small panel first, so if you are going to junk a dented mudguard, use it to practise on before consigning it to the bin.

The curved lip on the edge of the floor and legshields suffers badly on Vespas, as it is vulnerable to every knock. Fortunately, it is fairly easy to get back into shape.

04.57 Legshield denting is common. This damage was caused by the scooter sliding down the road on its side.

04.58 Creasing is an even bigger problem when it is over a large area and in a highly visible spot.

HOW TO RESTORE CLASSIC LARGEFRAME VESPA SCOOTERS

04.59 Roughly knock back the steel to begin with, then, using more care and a dolly, bring it back to the original shape.

04.61 Large deep dents are probably easier to deal with.

04.60 Make use of items like this indicator unit to check how things are progressing. Legshield shape can be gauged by offering up the outer trim if it is the solid type.

04.62 Start by knocking the panel down against a solid surface, watching and feeling the metal as you work.

04.63 The main dent should now be well on its way back out, but it's likely that the steel will have been pushed too far in places. Run a dual action sander over the surface; this will show the low spots where there is still paint remaining, and also the high bits that will become well polished.

04.64 Use a flat-faced body hammer and a dolly, working from side to side knocking in and out until the steel is reasonably flat. If you have trouble gauging it spray some satin black paint on the front face and sand off once more to get an idea of the high and low spots. Use a thin skim of filler to level off.

04.65 The lip at the edge of the legshields can be straightened using a large blunt chisel as a dolly and hammering roughly back into shape.

FRAME

04.66 Once the rough shape is made, final finishing can be done using some round bar or a drill bit to achieve the exact curvature.

SIDE PANELS/MUDGUARDS/ TOOLBOX

If your bolt-on panels are badly damaged, replacement is often a more sensible option than repair. If you have a PX, new side panels are readily available in both internal (cheap and easy to find) and external (more expensive and harder to locate) fitting. The Sprint series of scooters is covered with the exception of the Rally, although remanufactured versions for that model are supposedly on the way. The VBB type and the 8 inch wheeled Super have Indian Bajaj panels available as well as remade stuff.

The Piaggio, LML and Bajaj pressings are all pretty good, as you would expect. The remanufactured versions vary and may require work before being ready to fit, as some are machine stamped but hand-finished – a process that leaves small ripples and dents in the surface. Remade mudguards can also be variable in the accuracy of their pressing and often come un-drilled for the side mounts. Tool boxes and lids are remade too.

04.67 The side panels on pre-PX EFL scooters are held by these clips, which are released by pulling and twisting clear of the metal lug on the panel itself.

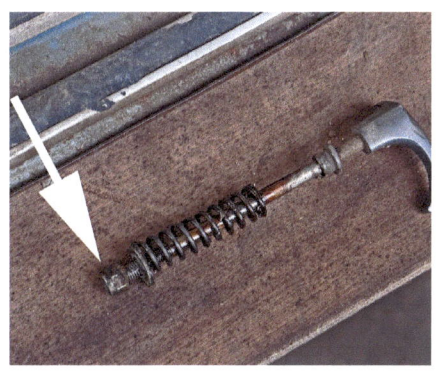

04.68 They are held inside the frame cavity by a locking nut (arrowed). Its position will also determine the amount of tension on the spring.

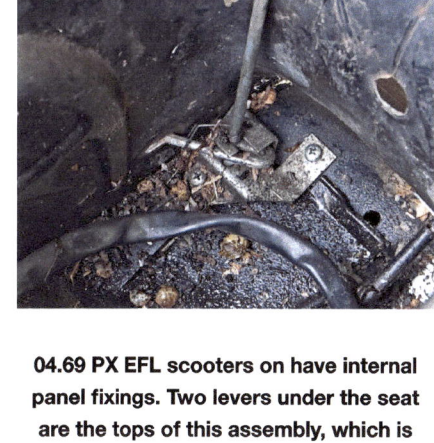

04.69 PX EFL scooters on have internal panel fixings. Two levers under the seat are the tops of this assembly, which is held inside the frame by self-tapping screws. Once the screws are undone the whole lot has to be manoeuvred out of the frame, which is a little tricky.

04.70 Panel damage is common, as is rusting, especially at the rear and around the mounting pin.

04.71 Expect to find more damage once the panels have been blasted or stripped. This one is torn as well as distorted.

04.72 Panels can be repaired by welding just like the main frame. Here, for example, the distorted section has been built up with weld then ground to an approximate shape, ready for filler.

HOW TO RESTORE CLASSIC LARGEFRAME VESPA SCOOTERS

04.73 The same panel is also covered in a variety of dents, the majority of which will need dressing out before moving on to the filler stage.

04.74 Sometimes a replacement makes more sense – it is always a balance between time, money and availability. New side panels can be sourced for VBB, Super, Sprint and PX early and late types. Rally versions are supposedly on their way.

04.75 Panels such as mudguards definitely do not warrant too much time being spent on them, especially when in this state. Replacements are inexpensive, although they may not be drilled ready for mounting. (See trim and front end chapters for details.)

04.76 Just because a panel is new, though, doesn't mean the work is over. This mudguard had a shallow dent that needed filling before paint went on.

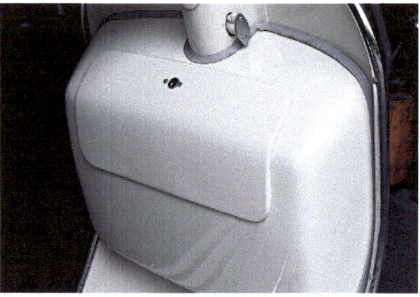

04.77 Toolboxes suffer damage from rust and accidents too. Copies are available, although a decent secondhand one may be a possibility. They all attach to the frame in a similar fashion, with screws either through the legshields or trapped in special plates welded to them. Replacement doors are also available for some models.

BRAKE PEDAL

04.78 Pre-PX scooters used a brake pedal like this. The pedal pivots around a pin welded to the frame, which is often seized if the scooter has been standing for any length of time. Apply releasing oil and try to get it all moving.

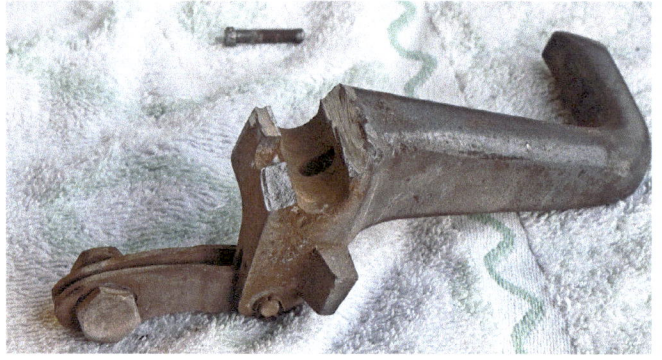

04.79 Once the brake cable is released at the wheel end, in theory the pedal should turn enough to give access to the securing pin (in background) that is removed from the underside. This is difficult to do when everything is in perfect condition, and almost impossible when it has been undisturbed for years. In many cases like this one the only way to get the pedal off is to cut it free from its pivot. Replacements are cheap and readily available in either standard or polished form.

FRAME

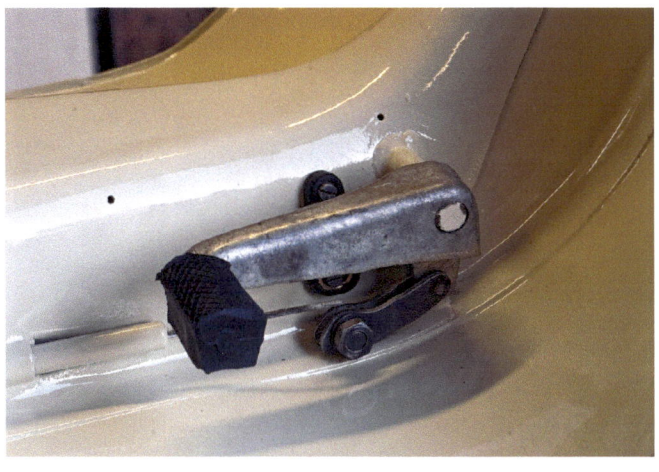

04.80 Refitting is easy when it is all new and clean. The shouldered pin goes in from the top.

04.81 The PX rear brake assembly is attached to the floor by nuts and bolts. Once undone the assembly can be pulled free from the chassis, assuming the brake cable has already been undone at the wheel end.

04.82 If a new floor has been fitted, there is a drilled hole where the pedal bolt will fit. It needs to be filed square, as it holds a captive nut whose sides sit on the lip of the floor.

04.83 The PX brake switch is held by a single bolt, if it needs replacing. The cable eye is held by a pin that often seizes, as does the main pivot pin, which causes the rear brake to stick. In theory these can be driven out, cleaned and reassembled, but a complete replacement may be a good idea as they are inexpensive, and modern road conditions and ineffective brakes are a bad mix.

CABLES

All the Vespas in this book rely on Bowden cables to operate essential controls, which are cheap and simple but suffer from corrosion, so wholesale replacement during the restoration is sensible. The cables on the market vary in quality and often in length, the best being nylon lined, which are also the most expensive. Cable ends are often poorly made on cheap versions, preventing them from sitting correctly in adjusters, and their outer sheaths are not usually a correct colour or texture match to Piaggio's originals. Replacing cables is a bit of a pain thanks to the internal construction of the central tunnel, where it kicks up with the legshields away from the floor. There are two options. The first is to run a guide cable down through the frame from the top – a length of thick electrical wire will do – then attach the new cable outer to it with tape, then pull it through the frame from the back end. Greasing the joint and the front few inches of the new cable can aid progress. The second option is simply to insert the cable outers from the top, again having greased the leading few inches, and push and jiggle until they are past the frame obstruction and through to the back end.

HOW TO RESTORE CLASSIC LARGEFRAME VESPA SCOOTERS

04.84 Cables can be fed through the frame from the top. Grease the ends to encourage movement. They sometimes stick where the tunnel starts to curve upwards, but a short pull back and a quick push will usually see them through the restriction.

04.85 Rear brake cables are a straight push through on a PX. Earlier scooters need the cable feeding into a tube. Fortunately there's enough room to get an arm into the frame cavity and 'feel' the cable into place.

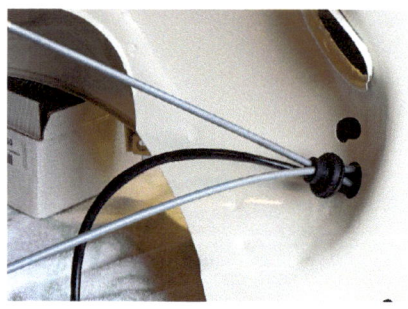

04.86 Wherever cables and wiring come through the frame, replace the rubber grommet that protects them.

STEERING LOCKS

Sprint and PX EFL-on types are shown in the pictures. VBB locks are straightforward to replace with the forks out of the frame – simply unscrew the outer retaining ring and pull the assembly into the steering stem cavity, and then lift it out. Pre-EFL PXs are very similar to the Sprint, and removal and replacement of the lock barrel is essentially the same.

Pre-PX Motovespa steering locks are different to Italian ones, with the locating pin in a slightly different location. New locks are therefore harder to find and more expensive.

04.87 Steering locks are all pretty similar on earlier scooters, pre-PX.

04.88 Knock off the cover with a hammer. Hopefully the securing rivet will come with it, otherwise it will have to be drilled out.

04.89 Pre-EFL PXs have a similar lock assembly, but without the flap.

04.90 Drill out the centre of the lock. Start with a small size, then move to a larger one.

04.91 Once you have drilled down through the tumblers, insert a screwdriver blade (arrowed) and twist and pull on the remains. There may be a spring under the barrel (not all models) – fish it out for re-use.

FRAME

04.92 There will not be a lot left of the old barrel once it has been drilled out. Clean any swarf out of the hole in the frame.

04.93 Replacement assemblies are cheap, although ones for Motovespa are different and are about three times the price of locks for Italian models. The raised square section (arrowed) comes in two sizes, so check before ordering a replacement.

04.94 The new barrel, which should be greased, is inserted with the key and spring, where fitted. It is automatically held in place by a pin once the key is removed – the barrel may need turning slightly for it to engage. If the barrel will not slide fully home, try turning the forks as you push it into place. A new flap is held in place by the rivet, and tensioned by the amount it is driven in.

04.95 The steering lock on the PX EFL-on is accessed from under the horn cast (see trim section for removal details), and has an electrical socket on the back. The socket is held in the tube by a grub screw (arrowed), and at the other end the wiring goes into a multi plug just below the lock. The grub screw is often rusty and seized, and may have to be drilled out.

04.96 There is a hole (arrowed) on the underside of the lock tube, and if you insert a thin pick or screwdriver you can push down a tumbler and pull the lock barrel out of the tube.

04.97 This is the tumbler – unfortunately it is sometimes stuck, as in this case. If so, the barrel can be driven out from the electrics side once the plug and the steering column locking ring is removed.

HOW TO RESTORE CLASSIC LARGEFRAME VESPA SCOOTERS

04.98 The locking ring looks like this. It sits immediately behind the electrics plug. It can be rotated and pulled free using a pair of long-nose pliers, although it too is often reluctant to pull free. Use a lot of lubricating spray and wiggle it about; it will come out eventually. The stuck barrel can be driven out from this side with a suitable drift.

04.99 If you had to drill out the electric plug locating screw, file off any burrs before attempting reassembly. Clean out the whole of the steel tube, removing any swarf or old grease.

04.100 Replace the steering lock ring after lubricating it, making sure that the centre T-shaped projection is facing towards the end of the tube where the electric plug will sit. The ring will just sit loosely in place for the moment. Secure the electric plug with a new grub screw that has been greased. The steering lock ring can now be pushed into place from the other end, with the T-piece locating into the plastic plug.

04.101 The main barrel is held by a sprung metal tang, which locates in a groove in the side of the barrel itself.

04.102 The outside cover ring, the barrel, and the locating tang can all be pushed into place together, and will locate with a click.

Chapter 5
Paint

DECISION TIME
Rightly or wrongly, most people are going to judge the quality of a restoration on how good the finished scooter looks, and with so much metalwork on show the paint finish is critical. The restoration bill for any Vespa is likely to be fairly hefty, and if there is to be any chance of recouping the investment then the finished scooter has to be attractive to potential buyers.

Learning to paint is not that hard; learning to paint *well* is a different matter altogether, so this may be one part of the rebuild where handing it over to someone else is a good idea.

Before you do pass the job to a third party, get some references and look at your chosen shop's recent work. Make sure that you get a firm quote and that it includes final finishing, so all the little imperfections are sorted by the person doing the paint before the top coats go on, and there is no excuse for it not being perfect.

COLOUR CHOICE
The range of Vespa colours can be found in *Vespa Tecnica Volume 6*, which includes paint swatches, but unfortunately the book is extremely expensive and probably not worth the investment unless you have a particularly rare variant and are committed to a factory fresh rebuild. Most paint shops should be able to mix a colour close enough to the original to satisfy most people (and in reality there were variations in hue during production, so it is very hard to prove exactly what is original in the first place). Factory paint codes can be found easily on dozens of websites, so there is no point listing them all here. The alternative is to find an unfaded part of your scooter – inside the headlamp shell for instance – and take that part to the paint shop for matching. Vespa colours are often very close to FIAT shades of the same era.

PAINT CHOICE
The situation regarding automotive refinishing products is rather confused in the EEC at present. In theory, high solvent paints are no longer to be used for vehicles, with water-based coatings having taken over. However, this type of paint is of no use to the DIY user at the moment, as it requires a heated booth, but that may change with time. Two-pack gloss is still around, often with a sticker attached saying 'not for automotive use.' It is definitely not suitable for home use, regardless of availability as it is highly toxic. This leaves cellulose as a realistic option, which can be legally sold for use on 'classic' vehicles. Some paint factors still offer a mixing facility to colour code with cellulose, but their number is dwindling fast. Others only have a small range of pre-mixed colours, so some homework on the local situation will be required. Another possibility is to use a two-pack base coat that does not contain isocyanate, and is therefore as 'safe' as cellulose, then use a one-pack clear lacquer to cover it. This method gives good results, but is less forgiving of mistakes than cellulose.

HOW TO RESTORE CLASSIC LARGEFRAME VESPA SCOOTERS

WHAT YOU NEED TO DO IT YOURSELF

The obvious requirement is somewhere safe to do the work, which means a well ventilated space free from any possible source of ignition (paint fumes are potentially explosive), and well lit by sealed fluorescent tubes. It also needs to be situated well away from your or anyone else's house. The cost of the hardware has to be taken into account as well. A compressor of at least 2hp with a 50-litre holding tank, air line, a water trap, regulator, a professional quality mask and a spray gun are all going to be needed just to get started. If you have all this gear, great; if not, investing in it is only worthwhile if you intend to restore more than one scooter, otherwise it is cheaper and easier just to get someone else to do the painting. Hiring the equipment is an option, but may not be particularly cheap, and the stuff tends to be larger than needed for DIY use.

It is possible to paint your scooter outside if you are using cellulose paint, as it dries very quickly. If that's your intention, choose a still day with no breeze and no strong sunshine, or the paint will dry before it hits the surface. The whole process will also prove irresistible to insects, especially with colours like yellow. Their remains will have to be flatted out after spraying.

PREPARATION

The glossy top coat is really the least of your problems. All the hard work comes beforehand, making sure that the surface is smooth and flat so that no imperfections are magnified by that lovely shine. This preparation is time-consuming and pretty dull. It is also a good idea to get a second opinion once you think the surface is good enough, as it is all too easy to settle for second best when your fingers ache from sanding, so ask a friend to be critical of your efforts.

FILLER

A bit of a dirty word to many, but body filler is an essential tool in preparing your scooter. It is designed to be used as a final thin finishing layer, not bunged into deep holes to cover up major damage. If you have done your panel bashing correctly, then this stage of the process should only involve a quick skim. Use professional quality stuff; cheap filler is too heavy to work with and usually very tough to knock back down. Buy one labelled 'easy sand' – it will be worth the small amount of extra cash. When rubbing down use a block, as it helps keep things level. If that isn't possible and a Vespa is pretty curvy, try to hold the paper with your fingers at 90 degrees to the direction of flatting, which will help prevent grooves being inadvertently rubbed into the surface. If it is difficult to judge whether the filler is even, spray on a light coat of satin black paint and flatten off once again. Low spots will stay black.

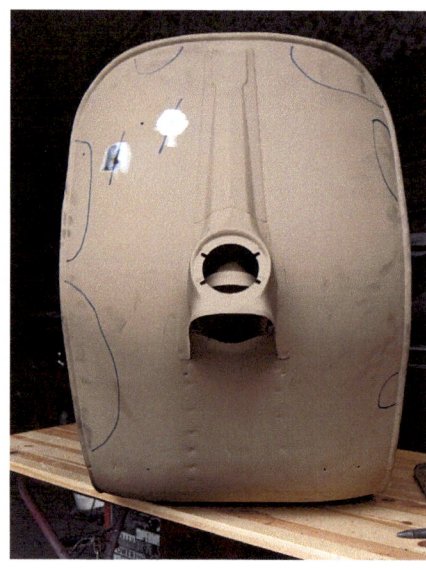

05.1 Pre-paint preparation begins by identifying the areas that will require filling to level the surface.

05.2 Filler should be good quality, or sanding will take forever. Large tins offer the best value, but the contents go off over time, so this benefit will be lost unless you make full use of the tin.

05.3 Filler needs to be spread over a large area to give enough room for the edge to be feathered out. This floor repair, for instance, needed to be taken high into the legshield to get a smooth transition over the welded repair, despite the join being well ground down.

PAINT

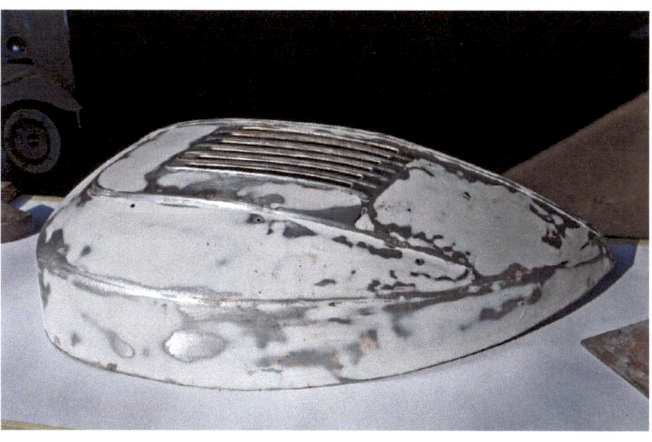

05.4 This side panel has all the imperfections filled, but unless done perfectly the edges of the repairs will show through the primer and paint.

05.5 If the whole area is covered a completely new level is created, which makes the levelling process a lot easier. The filler does not need to be thick – the finest skim is enough.

WORKSHOP AND PERSONAL PREPARATION

After the filling stage there is likely to be a lot of dust hanging around. Pop a mask on and, having wet the workshop floor, go round the frame and panels and blow them off. Do the same with all the other surfaces in the area including rafters and ledges. Give it a couple of hours to settle, sweep out the workshop, and then do it all again. Leave the floor damp but not wet when spraying, as it will keep down any residual dust and falling overspray.

Paint fumes of all types are a health hazard. Always wear a dedicated mask and surgical gloves to protect your skin. Your paint supplier will be able to provide the most appropriate versions – a simple dust mask from a hardware shop isn't good enough. Always vacate the area as soon as possible once you have finished, and do not return until the overspray has dropped. Even if the air seems clear keep your mask on, as particles and fumes linger for some time after, although they may not be visible to the naked eye.

NEW PANELS

Some remanufactured panels are supplied in bare metal and are greased or oiled for storage. Remove the grease with Panel Wipe – apply it generously and wipe off with lots of paper towels. Pay particular attention to folded seams. It is really hard to get rid of all the residue in one go, so leave the panel for a few hours then come back and do it all again. Run over the new panel with a dual action sander and an 80s disc to rough up the surface slightly before etching. If the panel came with transit primer on it, which is usually black, sometimes a light grey, it too needs sanding off before etching, as it is not usually a reliable enough surface just to paint over. It may also have imperfections and runs as it will have been applied quickly after manufacture.

05.6 Some new panels are greased rather than primed, which, frankly, is a pain. Clean them thoroughly with panel wipe, changing the paper often.

05.7 It is also advisable to roughen the surface with a sander before applying the etch coat, to help adhesion.

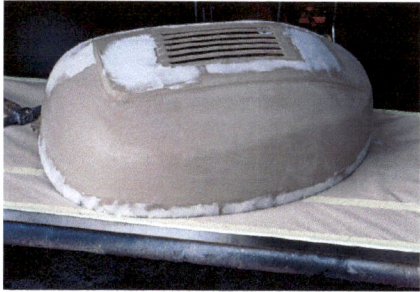

05.8 Once etched there will be enough contrast in the surface to detect any defects. This was a good pressing, but still needed a decent amount of filler to hide marks and spot weld depressions.

HOW TO RESTORE CLASSIC LARGEFRAME VESPA SCOOTERS

MASKING OFF

Buy proper masking paper from a paint supplier. Newspaper is temptingly cheap, but the ink can smear when subjected to thinners. If paint is being applied to a partially stripped scooter there is super-thin plastic sheet sold on a roll, which is perfect for moulding into even the tightest of corners.

ETCH (AGAIN)

If etch primer was applied earlier in the restoration after frame blasting, then lots of it will probably now be missing if welded repairs or dent removal have been carried out. Now is the time to completely re-cover the metalwork. In theory filler should not need it, but you might as well go over the whole lot. If you use a spray gun to apply the etch then the coat can be a little heavy due to the nature of the product, so once dry it is best if you leave it 24 hours, then flat it with some fine production paper to get rid of any 'orange peel.'

PRIMER

Apply at least three good coats of primer, allowing each to flash off slightly before adding the next. The period between coats is short with cellulose, and if you are painting all your frame and body panels in one go, by the time you have worked right round them all it will probably be time to do it again. Unless you are in a terrible hurry, leave the primer for 24 hours to fully harden. Now go over the whole lot with a guide coat in satin black. Once it has dried (ten minutes should do unless it is very cold in the workshop) flat the surface with 600s wet-and-dry sandpaper, which despite the name is always used wet. Keep the surface well wetted, and lubricate the paper with a little hand soap added to the water. Wash off the panels and allow to dry. There may be some white residue left behind – if so, wipe it off with paper towel before it hardens. Inspect the surface very carefully; there will almost certainly be some flatting marks or other minor imperfections unless your pre-paint preparation was excellent. Use stopper to fill these defects, and allow a further 24 hours for shrinkage before flatting back to the final surface.

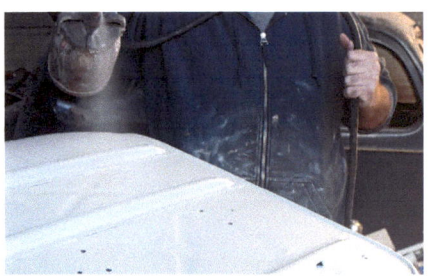

05.9 Once the filler is smooth a couple of coats of primer should be applied.

05.10 When dry, the primer should be covered with a guide coat of satin black aerosol. It only needs to be dusted on.

05.11 Rub down the guide coat with 600s paper, used very wet and lubricated with a little soap. Note that fingers should be at right angles to the direction of travel where possible to prevent accidentally introducing ridges in the surface.

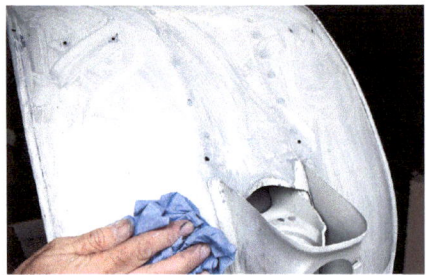

05.12 Any residue should be wiped away whilst still wet. All of it has to go, or further paint coats will not adhere to the surface.

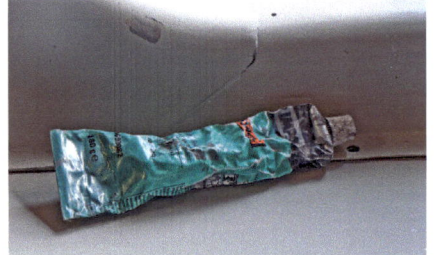

05.13 Once completely clean, the surface should be examined again. Unless you are very lucky (or good) there will be minor imperfections such as sanding marks or small air bubbles in the filler. These are best removed by applying stopper. Cellulose-based stuff in a tube is cheap and easy to use.

05.14 Apply the stopper thinly – your paint shop may sell small foam spreaders just for this job, but otherwise use a fingertip. The stopper air dries and shrinks in the process, so add more than you initially think is needed, and leave for 24 hours before sanding down. If removal is attempted too early, the surface will just roll up under the paper.

PAINT

SEALER

It makes sense to seal gaps in panels on the frame, especially on the underside where they will be subjected to road spray, unless you are intending to enter the restored scooter into concours competitions where complete originality is expected. The join between the floor and tunnel can be sealed too, as rust starts in the gap and staining results. If done carefully it is all but invisible to the naked eye.

05.16 Pull away the tape carefully whilst the sealant is still wet to leave the gap sealed but not intruding into the floor. Once painted, this seal will not be noticeable unless the joint is inspected very closely.

PRIMER AGAIN

Once the stopper and sealant have been done, prime again with a couple of coats. Once dry, gently rub down with 600s wet-and-dry paper, which should leave a smooth, blemish-free surface ready for the shiny stuff. Carefully clean any residue then wipe the surface with a tack rag, which will pick up any lingering dust or debris.

TOP COATS

The correct ratio for cellulose is 50 per cent paint to 50 per cent thinners. Use dedicated top coat thinners, not the standard stuff, which is only suitable for primer and cleaning your gun. Anti-bloom thinners should be used in damp conditions, although it is getting harder to find now. Apply at least five coats, which will give a decent amount of paint to cut back if there are any problems. The final top coat should have the thinners ratio increased to 65 per cent, which will enhance the shine, but also the probability of getting runs, so exercise caution when putting it on.

Use proper mixing cups and a measuring stick to mix the paint. Before applying the top coats give the spray gun and air line a final wipe

05.15 The joint between the floor and the central tunnel traps moisture and corrosion starts easily here. Line the edges of the joint with tape as closely as possible and squeeze in a thin bead of automotive sealant, not household stuff, which can actually accelerate rust.

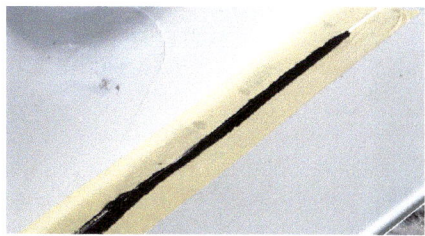

05.17 Seal any joints on the underside of the scooter, too. It will help stop water creeping between panels.

05.18 Some people like to make sure that their frame numbers are not obscured by a heavy coat of paint. If that seems like a good idea just tape them off before applying the top coat, removing the tape whilst the paint is still tacky. If it is left until the paint hardens there is a risk that the new surface will lift away along with the tape.

down, just to make sure there's no lingering dust. With the gun adjusted to give a spray pattern that resembles an upright rugby ball, keep the gun a hand's span away from the surface and apply the coats so that each pass of the gun overlaps the one already

05.19 With everything sealed and stoppered, add another two coats of primer and wet flatten. Clean the surface carefully, ready for the top coat.

laid down. When painting around curved sections, try and keep the gun distance steady to decrease the chance of running.

Lots of practice is the only way to learn paint application, and cellulose at least dries quickly and can be flatted back if mistakes are made.

FINISHING TOUCHES

Once the final coats are done, allow

HOW TO RESTORE CLASSIC LARGEFRAME VESPA SCOOTERS

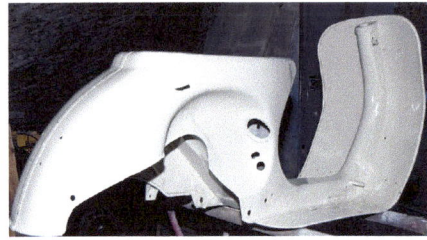

05.20 Unless you fabricate a stand for the job, the underside will have to be painted first, left to dry, then the top surfaces done.

05.21 New plastic parts need to be thoroughly degreased with panel wipe.

05.22 The cleaned surface has to be covered with an adhesion promoter or the paint will just peel off. It can be bought in aerosol form, which is handy as it is expensive stuff.

at least 24 hours (preferably longer) for drying then inspect the surface closely. Heavy runs or dry sections where there is insufficient paint will mean another round of sanding and repainting. If the defects are light – for example, if there is dust trapped in the surface or the paint is a bit dull – then flatten the surface with 1500s grade wet-and-dry paper, used wet with a little soap to ease progress, until it is all uniformly matt. Using a wet cloth, apply some buffing paste to one small section of the surface at a time, then polish off with a buffing machine. This can also be done by hand, but it is laborious work. The head of the buffer needs to be kept damp or the paint surface will burn. After buffing, the surface should be shiny, hard and smooth. Wipe off any remaining residue with a soft cloth, then apply a good quality automotive polish. The final job is to stand back and admire your handiwork.

PAINTING PLASTIC

If you are restoring a Vespa from the mid-1970s on, plastic will feature more frequently. Painting it does require a little more effort than steel, but is still possible in the home workshop.

SMALL PARTS

The techniques for painting smaller parts are exactly the same as used on the main frame and components. Remanufactured wheels often come with a very brittle and thin coating, so for long-term use repainting them is a good idea. The colour they are supplied in is often a poor match to the original Piaggio colour, which is another good reason to refinish them.

05.24 Self-painted rims will probably stand the test of time better than the supplied finish from the manufacturers, which can flake off all too easily.

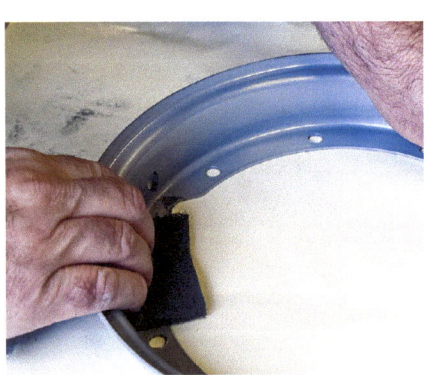

05.23 New wheel rims come painted, but if a change is desired the surface can be prepared with a Scotchbrite pad, which will matt it enough to give good adhesion.

05.26 Smaller panels can be supported on boxes or similar. Ensure they are stable enough to withstand the spray gun pressure. If attempting paintwork for the first time, starting with something like a mudguard is a good idea. There's less rectification work to do if it gets covered in runs.

05.25 Painting items like the bars and the headset may require a little lateral thinking and a degree of dexterity.

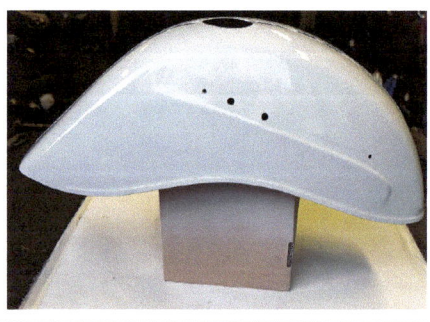

Chapter 6
Electrics

WIRING LOOM
Pre-PX

The wiring looms for these models follow the same basic pattern, with the main loom running through the frame tunnel, with spurs for the brake pedal and horn circuit. At the rear there are subsections for the back light, the engine electrics, and finally the battery or rectifier on the left where fitted.

The remains of the old wiring loom can be cut into suitable sections and simply pulled free of the frame. The new one should be installed from the tank space and drawn to the front using a guide wire. The brake and horn feeds can be loosely taped to the main loom before you start. Watch carefully for their arrival at their respective holes as the wiring is fed through, then pull them out and secure them to the frame, so that they do not disappear again as you get the wiring out at the headset. Alternatively, thread some draw wires through for these circuits as well as the main loom, and use these to pull the wires into place. The loom comes up through the cable slot in the frame on the right-hand side of the steering column tube, and can be a tight fit. Greasing the outer plastic sheath before fitting can ease its progress too.

The original loom will have a sub-loom running to the handlebar switch. Some non-genuine replacements have this incorporated into the main section, which makes the job considerably harder, so try to buy an original type – the job is irritating enough as it is without added complications. If the loom isn't pulling through the frame, it may be snagging on the lip where the spine bends upwards with the legshields. Try to get your arm inside the frame and push the loom forward as you pull at the headset, to encourage it past the obstruction. An assistant is useful here.

Other problems with many aftermarket looms are incorrect lengths of wire that need extra splicing in, plus either a complete lack of terminals or incorrect ones. Try to find someone who has used your proposed purchase recently, and make sure that it is up to scratch – internet forums are a good source of feedback. The alternative is to make your own loom using the original as a template – they really are quite simple on the 6-volt scooters, and everything from the right grade of wire to suitable connectors should be available off the shelf from a local auto electrician.

06.1 Replacement looms can be sourced for virtually all models. Quality and design vary markedly, so buy on recommendation if possible.

HOW TO RESTORE CLASSIC LARGEFRAME VESPA SCOOTERS

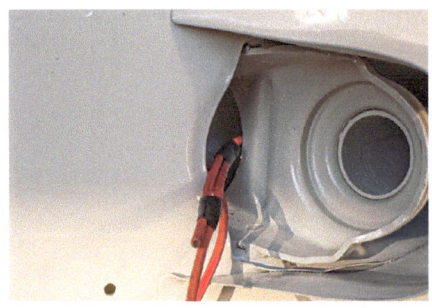

06.2 Getting the loom in place is easiest using a guide wire. This can sometimes catch on the inner frame strengthener. If it's a problem, thread it into the lower frame through the horn cast, out through the tank hole, and down the steering tube from the top, then join with tape and pull round until there is an uninterrupted length right through the frame.

06.3 The ends of loose wires, like these ones for the horn, can be taped to the loom temporarily to prevent them snagging as you pull it all through the frame cavity.

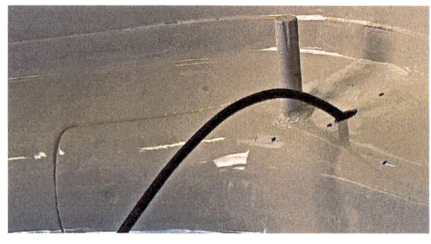

06.4 A separate guide wire for the small spurs may prove useful, as the holes they have to pass through are small.

PX

The PX loom is subdivided between the headset and the frame with a connector block behind the horn casting, which makes the process of replacing it all much simpler in terms of both the installation and reconnection, due to each circuit having individual and distinct connector plugs. This makes it impossible to get them mixed up. The installation process is pretty much the same as for the earlier models, using a guide wire to pull the loom into place.

Wiring diagrams

It would not be possible to reproduce all the wiring diagrams to cover the models included in this book. However, virtually all of them are freely available on the internet on specific scooter sites, and also on dealers' websites.

Wiring connections

Soldering is the best way to make connections. Previous attempts at repair which include crimped connectors should be removed if the loom is not being replaced, as they are a common source of problems. If crimping is your chosen method, then at the very least buy a decent hand tool – cheap ones are useless and will result in poor connections.

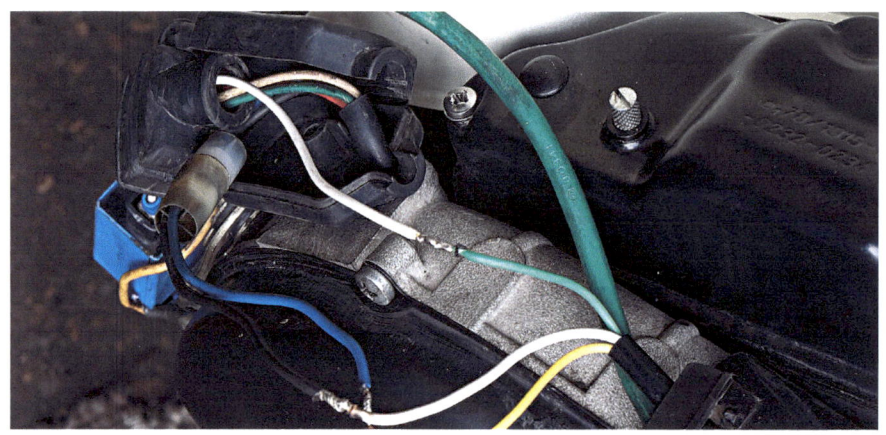

06.5 This is a conversion loom being fitted to a PX engine installed in an earlier frame. The plastic connector was re-used and the wires soldered to the originals, which were cut down. Soldering is superior to crimping. Use heat shrink sleeving or loom tape to cover the joints and bind the wiring together once finished.

06.6 PX looms are easier to fit despite being more complicated thanks to their use of multi-plug connectors with sub-looms feeding switches etc. Note the damaged wires on this starter motor inhibitor switch (arrowed). If the loom is to be retained, damage like this must be addressed.

ELECTRICS

HEADLIGHT

Headlights lose their internal silvering over time and then suffer from rust. Replacements can be found for almost all models, along with the appropriate bulb holder. The headlight bulb rating should not be altered as the electrical system is pretty finely balanced, and fitting a higher capacity bulb may just result in dimmer lights rather than the hoped-for improvement.

If a halogen bulb is fitted (PX disc models) you should only handle it by the metal base – never touch the glass. The bulb holder twists anticlockwise to release. Non-halogen units are held by two clips.

TAIL-LIGHT

Rear lenses are mainly plastic and held to the light body by two machine screws, which are often rusty. There should be a rubber seal between the lens and the main light unit. Replacement lenses and complete units can be bought, but again, the quality of some is dreadfully poor. Original lenses with light scratching or discolouration can sometimes be rescued by polishing the surface with some paint buffing compound. Lens screws should be greased before refitting, and not overtightened or the plastic can crack. The main light body is attached to the frame with self-tapping screws from under the wheelarch (PX), or with screws and nuts on earlier scooters.

INDICATORS

Most problems are caused by corrosion, either in the bulb holders or the earth (ground) connections. Wiring in the rear side panels can also fray unseen, as it is clipped out of the way – remove it and check the sleeving for wear if there is a persistent problem. The indicator relay is a black rectangular plastic box mounted in a rubber clip near the voltage regulator unit. Late PXs may have an audible indicator warning unit fitted – if it fails, replacement is the only answer.

06.7 Halogen headlights were fitted to disc-equipped PXs. They can be retro-fitted to EFL range scooters as long as the matching headlight sub-loom is also used. Never touch the glass on a halogen bulb – always handle it by the metal mounting.

06.8 New bulb holders are inexpensive, but may be poorly made. Even the better ones may require some work on the terminals and contacts before they will function reliably.

06.9 Unlike previous models, the P series rear light unit has to be removed from the underside at the rear.

06.10 P-range front indicator bulb holders are accessed from inside the toolbox. They are under rubber sleeves (white arrow), which can be pulled out of the way. The holders just twist to release. The main indicator body is held in place by two machine screws (yellow arrows). If the scooter is fitted with clear lenses from the factory, the orange-tinted bulbs have offset mounting pins.

HOW TO RESTORE CLASSIC LARGEFRAME VESPA SCOOTERS

06.11 Some markets had bar end indicators fitted to pre-PX models. As they were all 6-volt versions they were not very bright or particularly reliable. Replacements – either genuine Hella or copies – are readily available, and have a definite retro charm if nothing else.

06.12 Rear indicators on the P series scooters take their feed through this mushroom-headed connector in the end of the front locating pin. It needs to be clean and shiny.

06.13 The rear units earth (ground) through a strap that passes to a bolted connection (arrowed) on the inside of the wing, which is often corroded, causing problems.

SWITCHGEAR/INSTRUMENTS/ BRAKELIGHT SWITCH

The wiring to the switchgear suffers from the usual corrosion found elsewhere on any old scooter, but the left-hand grip on a PX (and earlier models in some markets fitted with an indicator switch) has an additional problem, as the movement when changing gear can eventually break the connection between the wires and the switch. If the wiring to the switches is sound, but a problem persists, replacement is the only long-term solution as they cannot be reliably disassembled.

Instrument lighting is basic pre-EFL PX, normally a single festoon bulb whose holder often corrodes. Later scooters and the T5 MkI use a flexible printed circuit board that goes brittle over time and then suffers from internal breaks, which mean complete replacement to rectify any problems. Dash lighting on these models is by automotive-style bulb holders, which you twist anticlockwise to remove.

Fuel gauges are temperamental and their sender units wear out. The latter can be replaced cheaply, but a new speedo head will be needed to rectify the former. Indian versions are commonly found for sale on the web, but are not a direct copy. This is especially true of the ones being sold as T5 MkI.

The brakelight switch on pre-PX scooters is held in place by a pair of screws. There should be a rubber seal between it and the frame. The wiring

06.14 PX left-hand switches suffer from the wiring pulling free. Re-soldering the joint may do the trick.

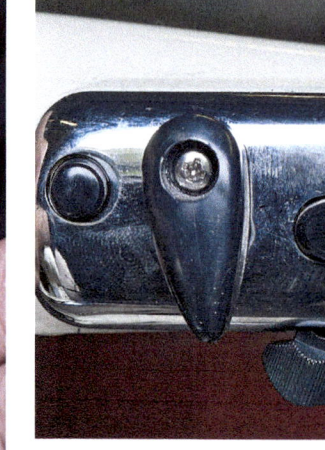

06.15 Earlier switches are robust, but if they are faulty replacement is the only real solution. Quality can be an issue with remanufactured versions.

may be crimped directly to two plates or by a pair of bullet connectors. PX switches are held in place by a single bolt, accessed once the pedal assembly has been dropped from the frame.

ELECTRICS

06.16 EFL and later warning lights are automotive-style, combined bulb and holder units. The speedometer light is a push fit into a circular hole and has a separate bulb.

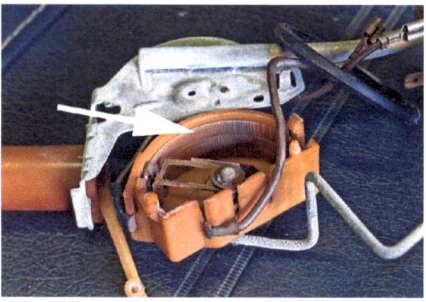

06.17 Fuel sender units wear through the wiring track (arrowed) and cannot be repaired. New units are not too expensive.

06.18 Pre-PX brakelight switches rely on two plates making contact. Soldering the wiring in place is more secure than using bullet connectors.

HORN

Pre-PX all the horn units simply screw into the horn cast with a rubber sealing ring underneath them. PX versions are accessed by removing the separate plastic horn cast that gives access to the unit, which is held in place by two screws. Replacements for all types are available, but cheap ones usually have appalling chrome. 6-volt horns will continue to work if the scooter is converted to 12-volt, as they are used infrequently and so will tolerate short bursts of higher voltage.

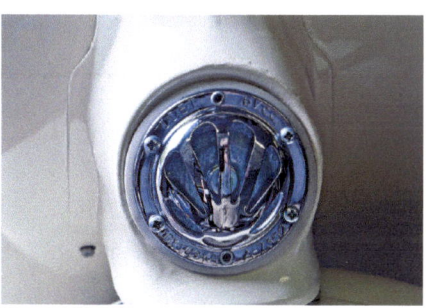

06.19 Replacement horns often have poor chroming. A good quality European one like this is surprisingly expensive.

06.20 PX horns are screwed into the rear of the plastic horn cast. Replacement is simple.

IGNITION
Points system

There is nothing inherently wrong with a points setup, as long as the components are in good condition. The points may be one piece, in which case the base plate screw allows their removal. If not, there will be a spring clip to remove first, which will allow the moving half to lift away, giving access to the base plate and the securing screw. They are adjusted by either an eccentric screw or by slots in the plate, depending on type. Access is through a hole in the flywheel. The points gap should be 0.012-0.020in for P125/150X, and 0.011-0.019in for previous models.

06.21 Points stators are all pretty similar. This one, a VBB type, has damaged slots (blue arrow), poor wiring, and generally looks very tired. A replacement is the best option. These points are one piece. If there was a larger clip here (green arrow) it could be removed to allow the moving section of the points to lift free. The removable clip type is most common on Sprint era scooters.

06.22 The points will have a connector (arrowed) to the ignition coil on the stator. Make note of the position of any isolating washers fitted – incorrect reassembly will result in the loss of a spark.

HOW TO RESTORE CLASSIC LARGEFRAME VESPA SCOOTERS

06.23 The points are adjusted by loosening the base screw (green arrow), and moving the base plate left or right with a screwdriver levering the posts (white arrows) as required.

06.24 The points are inexpensive, so replace them automatically on a rebuild. The faces (left arrow) should be cleaned before fitting, as a preservative is often used on them. This plastic end runs on the flywheel. There is a felt lubricating pad (right arrow) built into the stator; make sure that it is oiled, or the heel of the points will wear rapidly.

06.25 The condenser is held by a single screw (or a push fit on P models), and its wiring is soldered in place on top. Again, an automatic replacement on a rebuild.

06.26 P series points look different but follow the same system as the earlier versions, with a screw connector for the wiring (bottom arrow) and a soldered joint at the condenser (top arrow).

06.27 The points themselves are very compact, and bear a strong resemblance to Fiat car versions of the same era.

Ignition timing

Two-stroke engines in general are sensitive to changes in ignition timing, and even those in a soft state of tune like standard Vespas benefit from it being set up accurately.

The best way to check the ignition timing on points-equipped models is to use a dial gauge when the engine is apart, but this is an expensive solution. An alternative is to use a piston stop to make a timing mark, which is much cheaper, then wiring up a light or simply using a cigarette paper to check exactly when the points open up in relation to that mark. The photos opposite show the budget method of checking it out.

The markings on the case are easiest done low down, as the flywheel is closest at this point. Once made others can be accurately added at a more convenient spot for later use on the flywheel housing, or even on the head cooling shroud which is useful for timing checks with a strobe light when the engine is running.

The points gap must be correct before any attempt to set the timing is made. Once it is, slip a cigarette paper between the faces of the points and turn the flywheel anticlockwise until the paper is trapped. Turn the flywheel clockwise again and the paper should just be coming free at the timing mark you created. If the paper is free before the mark is reached the timing is advanced and the stator plate needs to be moved clockwise by a small amount. This is all a matter of trial and error until the correct relationship is achieved. An alternative to the paper is a bulb and a battery so the earth (ground) is attached to the cases and a wire passes from the positive through the bulb terminals and on the points feed to the coil. The bulb will dim as it hits the timing mark and the points open: again, adjust the stator as required to get it right.

ELECTRICS

06.28 A top dead centre (stop) tool can be made at home using an old sparkplug with the porcelain and electrodes removed. A bolt is secured through the centre, protruding from the end of the threads. Make sure it is all done up tight, and screw back into the head.

06.29 Mark the end of one flywheel fin, then turn the crank until the piston touches the stop tool. Make a mark on the case opposite the marked fin. Turn the engine all the way back until it comes into contact with the piston stop again, and mark this position on the case as well.

06.30 A timing disc is needed next, either bought from your local scooter shop or downloaded from the internet, printed out, and glued to some thin card.

06.31 Trap the disc loosely between a washer and the flywheel nut (flywheel now removed) and use the markings to find the middle point of the two marks that you have just made – this is top dead centre (TDC). Tighten the disc and double-check the markings.

06.32 Notch the case with your TDC position and highlight it with paint. This middle point could also be determined by careful measurement as an alternative to a disc.

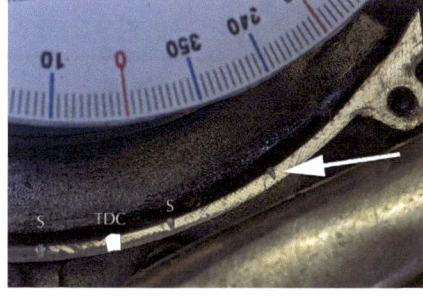

06.33 Using the disc lined up to TDC, count back the amount of degrees required for your particular model and make your firing point notch, so the final setup looks like this. The S marks are the two stop tool positions, TDC is exactly in the middle of them, and the timing point is arrowed. The flywheel turns in a clockwise direction when running so marks to the right of TDC are before TDC (BTDC), which is what is required.

Timing settings (before top dead centre)
VBB – 28 degrees
GL150 – 22 degrees
Sprint series including Rally 180 – 22 degrees
P125/150X – 21 degrees

Electronic system
The vast majority of electronic models have Ducati systems. A pick-up replaces the points on the stator and acts as the trigger to discharge the coil. Some Rally 200 models use Femsa ignition, which has acquired an unfair reputation for unreliability. Replacement parts for the system are expensive though, and often hard to get. It might be worth converting a Rally so that it's equipped to take Ducati electrics when the engine is being rebuilt. The swap requires a new crank, flywheel side bearing, stator plate, flywheel, regulator and CDi unit. It also brings the electrics up to 12-volt.

Some Spanish models have their own version of Femsa fitted. Parts for

06.34 Some PX models have a small protrusion on a flywheel fin (arrowed), which allows the use of a stroboscopic timing light to check the ignition. There are corresponding marks pressed into the metal of the cover.

HOW TO RESTORE CLASSIC LARGEFRAME VESPA SCOOTERS

06.35 On Ducati electronic stators the points are replaced by a pick-up box (arrowed). These are reliable, but any unusual misfires can often be traced back to this unit. It has one soldered wire connection and is secured by a screw that is usually very tight.

06.36 Conventional systems rely on simple coils. VBB era versions may be inside separate plastic covers. All bolt on in the same manner.

06.37 Electronic ignitions have this ignition unit in place of a straightforward coil. The built-in yellow wire is an earth (ground) – it often corrodes and breaks, but the unit will continue to work without it.

06.38 A forked metal HT lead end combined with a solid copper core lead gives reliable long-term service. The contact is made by this pin piercing the lead's shrouding. Crude but effective.

06.39 Modern resisted caps are fine, but the gap around them which allows hot air to escape under the side panel is less welcome.

these models are even harder to find, and the swap mentioned previously isn't possible as the castings differ slightly.

Ignition timing with either electronic setup is simply a matter of ensuring that the appropriate marks on the stator plate are lined up – see the engine overhaul chapter for details. It can be checked with a strobe light if there is any doubt.

Ignition coil

The design of the coils fitted to points-equipped scooters varied throughout production, but, regardless of type, replacement is probably sensible in any restoration due to age. Electronic ignition coils (commonly referred to as the CDI) are also freely available at a range of prices, genuine Ducati is the best bet for reliability although it comes at the highest price.

HT lead/sparkplug

The HT lead should be an immediate replacement along with its cap and a plug during any rebuild. Replacement leads are once again of variable quality. If bought by the length, make sure that the lead is cut down to the same size as the original – if it's too long it will rub on the inside of the side panel and short out.

The most basic setup is a copper core lead that screws into the CDI at one end, and at the other a simple forked prong held in a rubber boot, which fully covers the hole in the cylinder shroud. Original fitment suppressor caps are prone to being faulty and causing misfires, so should be replaced with the prong type. Aftermarket plug caps and carbon fibre leads do not really add much other than expense, and the gap left around the cap allows hot air out under the side panel, which Piaggio originally went to great lengths to prevent. The plug should be the one listed for your scooter and the environment it is going to be used in. NGK are a popular fitment, but for 125/150 models a B6HS is ideal for general day-to-day use. Step up to a B7HS where journeys include longer stretches of faster running. For continuous hard use a B8HS may be needed. 200cc and T5 models use a longer reach plug, B6ES, moving up to 7 and 8 as above where conditions dictate. The electrode gap should be 0.6mm.

CHARGING SYSTEM

On older Vespas with 6-volt systems poor lights and a weak spark are often accepted as simply par for the course, but the situation can often be significantly improved by having the flywheel re-magnetised. This is a cheap process, although finding someone able to carry it out may be more problematic. If you have acquired the scooter in bits and the flywheel has been stored separate from the stator for any length of time,

ELECTRICS

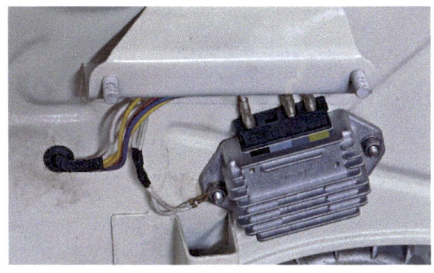

06.40 On PXs and most 12-volt conversions without a battery, the current is controlled by a 3-pin regulator like this. It is finned to allow the heat generated during use to dissipate quickly.

06.41 Models fitted with a battery will have a 5-pin version that acts as a rectifier as well as a regulator.

it will almost certainly need doing, and should be regarded as good practice even if everything has remained together – at least you then know one of the basics is right before launching into lighting coil replacements, etc.

Voltage regulation is controlled by the light switch on pre-PX scooters, with the tail-light bulb designed to blow to prevent the system being subjected to long-term damage. The PX uses a separate finned regulator mounted under the left-hand side panel. If it fails the headlight bulb will glow much brighter than normal and smaller bulbs will rapidly fail, alerting the rider to the problem. The unit is held by two screws and the wiring is colour coded. Note the earth (ground) wire that sits under one of the securing screws. If fitted, the battery tray will have to be removed to gain access.

Where a battery is installed the circuit is pretty much an add-on, and the scooter will continue to run even when it is discharged. Continuing to use it in this state is not advisable though as it can result in a heavy load on the stator. Running without a battery connected at all will damage the regulator in the long term.

STARTER MOTOR
The starter motor is held by three nuts and a bottom plate. The main wear is usually to the brushes, which are accessed by undoing the end cover (three screws). Parts are not easily found, but an auto electrician should be able to match up the brushes. New ones need soldering in place. If fitting an engine with electric start cases into an older scooter, the starter itself normally has to be removed or it will not fit. A rubber bung is available to block the empty starter hole, or alternatively, a more expensive metal plate, both of which stop dirt getting into the cooling system.

CONVERTING TO 12-VOLT
This is a worthwhile idea if the scooter is in regular use, but the possibilities are legion. If you are happy having 6-volt ignition and only want 12-volt lights (pretty much all models pre PX) then simply swapping the lighting coils on the original stator plate is the quickest method. A regulator from a PX will be required plus the light switch replacing along with all the bulbs. Complete stator replacement for a 12-volt type is the next alternative which requires the additional parts mentioned above plus a new coil. If you are willing to go this far, though, it may be better to buy one of the many kits on the market and have electronic ignition as well. These kits are often based on Indian Bajaj parts, which are decent quality, although copies and fakes are not unknown and these are obviously much less reliable.

Another option is to use a conversion kit from one of the

06.42 Starter motors come in two sizes, although the exact dates of fitting appear unclear. They are interchangeable, with the length of the support plate being the only difference when mounting them.

German suppliers, which comes with a crank and PX electrical parts and fits virtually all rotary valve models. This is good value if the crankshaft needs replacement during the engine rebuild anyway, and should be a reliable upgrade.

It may be that a complete engine swap was decided upon during the renovation, most commonly fitting a PX unit into an older scooter, like the Motovespa Sprint featured in these pages. If that is the case, replacement looms are available ready-made off-the-shelf from several sources, along with matching light switches. The rest of the electrical components will need replacing as outlined above.

All these conversions will require at least some wiring loom changes, but if the work is being done during restoration bespoke looms can be bought off-the-shelf for whatever setup you choose.

06.43 Swapping lighting coils is a simple and cost-effective upgrade to 12-volt lighting.

Chapter 7
Trim

BADGES/PANEL TRIM

Vespas were modestly priced vehicles, and as such were not over adorned with brightwork, which explains why there were so many aftermarket manufacturers offering owners the chance to personalise their scooter. Most original badge types have been remanufactured now, but quality is variable, so buying blind is a risk. Make sure that you check the distance between badge locating pins too, as these can vary even on items that appear identical.

If you own a Motovespa then the correct badging may not be easy to source, in which case welding the holes and re-drilling the legshields to suit what can be purchased may be the only option. Decisions on badging should be made before painting, so if any drilling is needed it's done before your shiny new top coat goes on.

Original badges and trim were made from low-grade alloys, and in most cases original parts will prove almost impossible or prohibitively expensive to restore, so replacement may be the only answer.

If the badge type relies on mushrooming a fitting moulded into the back to secure it, it can be tricky getting a really tight fit to the legshield. Bend the badge to the shape of the legshield or panel first (taking care, as some copies are brittle), then add a small amount of Sikkaflex or similar sealer/adhesive behind the badge. It will act as a cushion and take up small amounts of slack. Support the face of the badge with something that will not mark the surface and tap the securing pin with a ball hammer to mushroom the end over.

07.1 Badges suffer from corrosion and discolouration as they are made from a cheap base alloy. The peened over heads (arrowed) have to be drilled or ground off to free them from the frame.

07.2 Horn cast (steel version) badges suffer from chipping and fading. Reproductions of virtually all types are on the market. They can be attached by using a smear of Sikkaflex or similar on the back.

TRIM

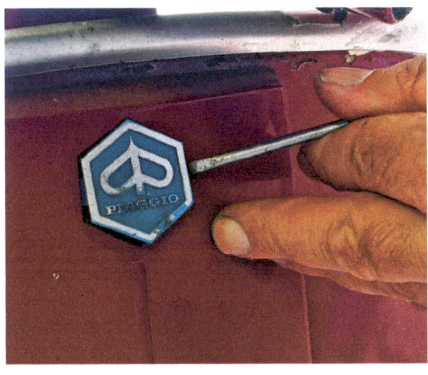

07.3 P series badges are plastic and suffer just as badly as earlier versions. They can be removed by carefully inserting a screwdriver underneath and pushing back the tag inside.

07.4 Modern Vespas have these adhesive badges which use the old script and are ideal for classic models. Remove the backing paper to expose the adhesive, position as required, rub down to ensure that it has stuck in place, then peel off the protective top layer of clear plastic.

07.5 Side panel badges also come in all types, although if you own something a little out of the ordinary like a Spanish Iris (bottom badge) you may have to look a little harder to find one.

07.6 Side panel badges are often held by small one-way clips on the rear. If they are a tight fit use a socket to drive them down into position.

07.7 The same type of fittings also secure alloy front mudguard crests. Discoloured ones can be cleaned with a soft wire brush or a buffing head fitted to a bench grinder. P series crests are plastic and secured by two self-tapping screws.

07.8 Alloy side strips on mudguards are held by these clips. The square bottoms slide into the channel pressed into the rear of the decorative strip. The strips usually have one short section that is separated from the rest of the channel by crimping. This must be used as your fixed reference point when measuring and drilling the mounting holes.

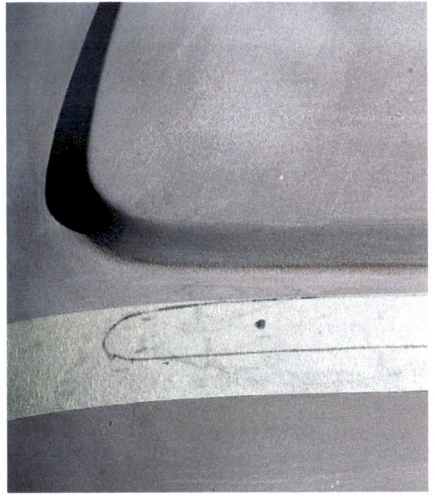

07.9 Side panel trim is the same as the mudguard. To attach it to a new panel, first stick some masking tape in roughly the right place, then lay the alloy strip on it. Once satisfied that it is positioned correctly, draw around the outside. Using that outline, mark the correct place for the holes to be drilled to secure it. Like the mudguard trim, two of the fittings will slide about over a large area, but the other is pretty much fixed. Make sure that you have factored that into your hole positioning.

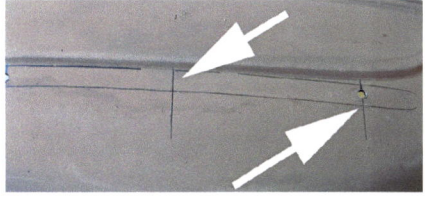

07.10 Drill your holes as required. Note the use of transverse lines to double check the accuracy of the positioning.

HOW TO RESTORE CLASSIC LARGEFRAME VESPA SCOOTERS

07.11 A flash of alloy on the panel really sets off the paint.

07.12 Floor trim pre-PX used alloy end caps riveted through the floor. The heads of the old rivets can be ground off from the underside, or drilled through and the remains removed with a punch.

FLOOR RUNNERS

In most cases replacement is the simplest solution. If the original runners are to be re-used, take care removing the old fixings – work from the underside of the scooter or you risk damaging the alloy. Slight tarnishing can be removed by using progressively finer grades of wet-and-dry paper until the surface is smooth. The new runners should be held in place with rivets, which are usually supplied as part of a kit. They are soft and the protruding shaft is supposed to have the end rounded to hold the runner in place. This is not that easy to achieve, and few people would relish wielding a hammer so close to newly and probably expensively applied paint. If absolute originality is the order of the day then rivets it has to be (and you will have to fabricate a concave-headed punch to mushroom the end for the correct factory look), otherwise one of the pictured alternatives is an easier and safer method. Stainless steel fitting kits with all the necessary nuts, bolts and washers are readily available.

The rubber trim strips need to be a tight fit, so it is better to cut them slightly too long and then force them in, otherwise over time the rubber shrinks back and leaves a gap. Some end caps will need the edge of the trim cutting away with a sharp knife in order to get a tight fit.

07.13 New alloy trim may look good in the packet but will need work before fitting, as an initial layout will show. The gap to the floor can often be remarkably large.

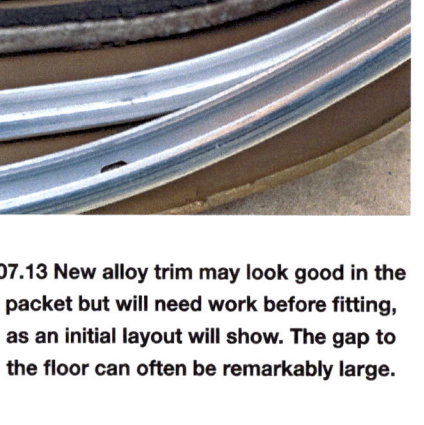

07.15 Other problems with the strips are poor finishing to the ends. This set had heavy burrs where they had been cut at the factory and around the rivet hole. Clean all of these defects with a file or you'll struggle to fit the trim correctly.

07.14 To get an accurate idea of how much bending is necessary and where, secure one end temporarily with a self-tapping screw. Now push the strip down and mark on it where the curvature is wrong. The strip can be bent and twisted by hand until a closer fit is achieved. It doesn't have to be absolutely perfect as the fittings will pull it down to a degree as they are tightened.

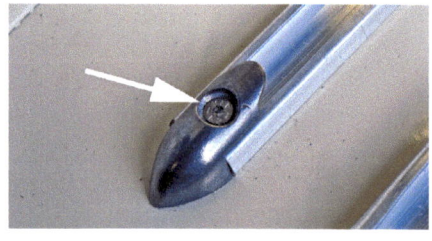

07.16 As an alternative to rivets, countersunk stainless screws can be used. M4 are usually recommended as they fill the hole in the cap better, but M3 may be an option (seen here) – although they sit a little lower, the exposed nut on the outside of the legshield is more discreet, being little larger than the original rivet head.

TRIM

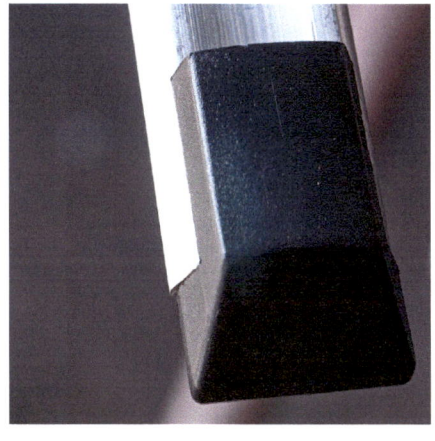

07.17 PX ends use these plastic caps which simply push into place, popping over the head of the rivet or screw to secure them.

07.18 The main run of the strips can be secured by dome-headed bolts, which will not interfere with the seating of the rubber trim.

07.19 Pop-rivets can used too, although their grip may be compromised where the floor trim is slotted. If that looks like being the case, use a slim washer under the rivet head. This rivet has been inserted from above, which makes fitting the rubber strip easier. It also means that the squashed end of the rivet is visible under the scooter. You could insert the rivet from underneath, again with the washer fitted to protect the alloy, though this would make fitting the rubber harder. The choice is yours.

07.20 If there is still some spring in the floor trim and you are relying on the fittings to hold it in place as discussed earlier, rivets may not be up to the job – the alloy may try to tear instead. To make sure that won't happen, gently clamp the floor trim down making sure that it is well supported, as shown here, then insert the rivet and fix in place. Screwed fittings should not need this extra assistance as they tighten more gently than pop rivets.

07.21 The shape of the rubber used pre-PX makes it tricky to fit, as it is reluctant to slide into position. If that is the case try putting one side into the alloy and pushing the other in place using a screwdriver. Care is required, as one slip could see you scratching any new paint.

07.22 Once in place, though, the new trims look great – the reward for a time-consuming and fiddly job.

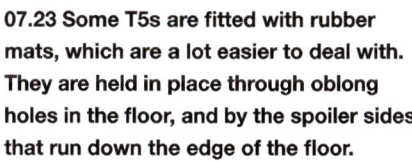

07.23 Some T5s are fitted with rubber mats, which are a lot easier to deal with. They are held in place through oblong holes in the floor, and by the spoiler sides that run down the edge of the floor.

07.24 Centre mats on older models and pre-EFL PX are secured by two trim strips held in place by rivets.

HOW TO RESTORE CLASSIC LARGEFRAME VESPA SCOOTERS

07.25 The mat rubber should be glued down as well. This can make getting the old one off rather time-consuming.

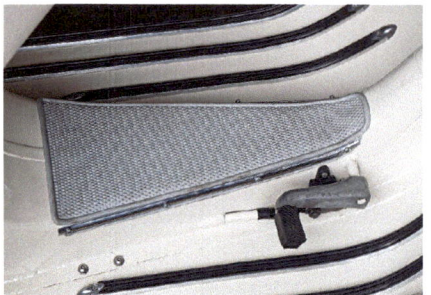

07.26 Replacing the mat is straightforward. Some may prefer to use stainless self-tappers to hold the rim in place rather than rivets. Either way, make sure that the rubber is squared up as you tighten the strips. Some aftermarket replacement strips are poorly drilled and the holes do not line up at all well, so expect to do a little work with a file elongating the holes if that is the case.

07.27 EFL PXs and later models have a solid plastic mat secured by four screws.

07.28 The old screws are often rusty with rounded heads, so just break away the plastic and get a pair of grips on them.

SEATS

The seats fitted to models covered by this book fall into three main categories: single seats that are metal sprung, dual seats also with springs, and double versions with moulded plastic bases. Decent copies of single seats are available as are covers to match, including remade versions of some famous aftermarket seats. The metal bands and cone springs used in the middle years are best replaced using universal kits usually marketed for use on Lambrettas, whilst the main framework can simply be cleaned and painted. Covers of various types can be bought, from original to fake snakeskin, but the main problem is the foam underneath the cover which degrades badly, losing its shape and density, and finally if exposed to the elements for any length of time, it becomes crumbly. At present replacement foam is rare, so the best and easiest option for most people is simply to buy a complete replacement seat. These come in a multitude of styles and colours, including accurate copies of most versions, but be careful about quality (as usual) as locks and/or catches are often poorly manufactured and hinges weak.

In theory, fitting a new cover is straightforward. If there is a rear badge fitted and/or a lock, start at the back, and once the new cover is approximately in place loosely fit the badge or lock through the appropriate holes. Pull the front of the cover into place next, then turn the set over and gently push it down as the cover is pulled up and into place. Roll the edge of the cover around the sides of the steel frame and secure with clips. New ones are readily available and cheap if the originals are too corroded to re-use.

The reality though may be radically different from the description above. Even using a good quality cover, expect to struggle pulling it down into position as it may be tight. Cutouts at the back may not have been accurately placed during manufacture so may need to be enlarged and the cover manipulated to ensure proper coverage of the lock hole. The cut at the sides may be overly generous and need trimming before wrapping around the edges of the frame or the excess will produce an unattractive bulge.

07.29 Metal sprung seats are simple in construction, relying on hooks and a couple of screws to keep everything in place.

07.30 The fittings can be tight and suffer from corrosion. Replacement kits may not be identical, but will do the job if the originals are unusable.

TRIM

07.31 If there are badges on the back of the seat, in this case a PX, they are normally simply screwed on.

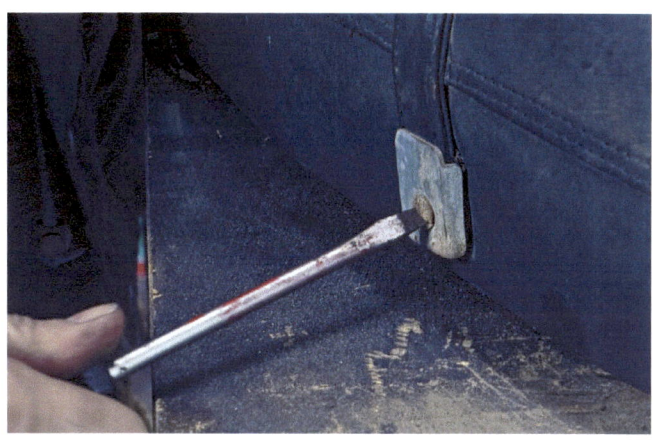

07.32 Seat straps are held by screws in plates on the inside of the seat. These too are often seized.

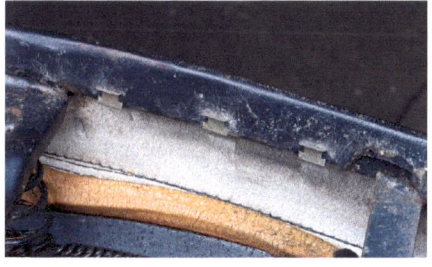

07.33 Steel-framed seats have these clips securing the cover. They simply push off.

07.34 Plastic-based seats use staples. They have to be prised out with a screwdriver.

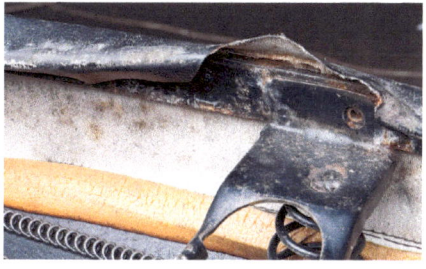

07.35 The old seat cover is rolled under the steel frame. It has to be worked free, or it could be cut with a knife to speed things up.

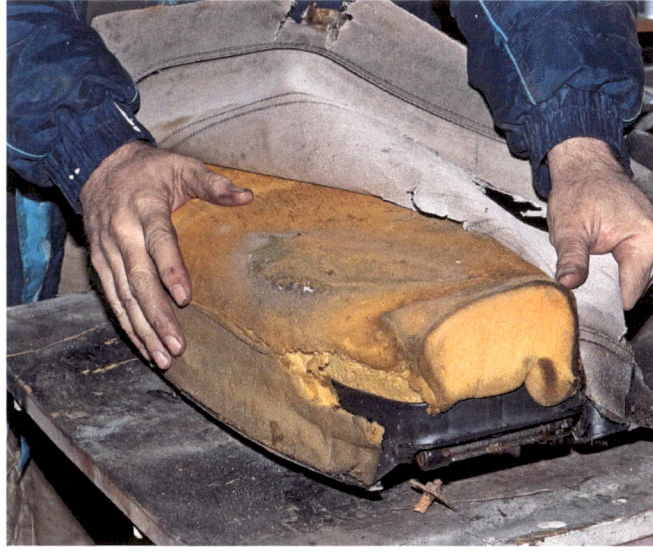

07.36 Once pulled off, expect to find damage to the foam underneath. This can be a major problem, as sourcing a replacement will prove difficult.

07.37 There may be a plastic base under the foam on some models (PX). If so, check for a locating strip stapled under the springs and remove it.

HOW TO RESTORE CLASSIC LARGEFRAME VESPA SCOOTERS

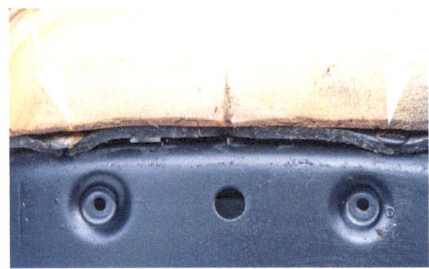

07.38 There may also be two plastic rivets at the rear. Prise these upward and out with a screwdriver.

07.39 The new seat cover may come with reinforcing sections already fitted to the front and rear. If not, re-use the originals. The cover is best fitted on a warm day, as it will be more flexible. If doing the job in the cold, warm the cover indoors for a short time, or even pop it in the tumble drier for a minute.

07.40 The cover needs to be under gentle pressure until the edges are rolled around the frame, or it will look saggy once finished. New clips may be supplied with the cover.

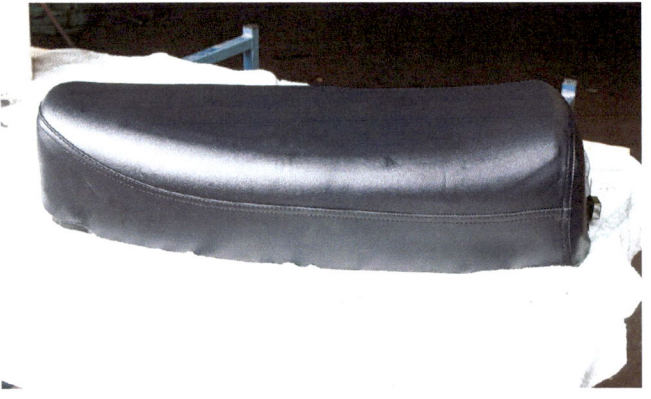

07.41 Once done the seat should look smooth. Minor marks or creases may still be apparent from its folded state, but these will soon disappear once it has been sat on a couple of times.

07.42 Replacement seats may have sticky or inaccurately made pin-locating mechanisms. Make sure that the spring-loaded section actually moves through its complete arc. It may also be necessary to elongate the slot at the top for the plate to close properly over the frame pin.

SPEEDOMETERS

Restoring an original speedo is difficult, as the ones fitted by the factory tended to be built to a very tight price, and time very much takes its toll. Replacement rims and glass (plastic) lenses may be available, but that may not be the end of the problem as inner faces tend to become sun-bleached and/or discoloured over time and there is little that can be done to rescue them. If an original plastic lens is yellowed then some gentle rubbing with a fine brazing paste will restore clarity although usually only for a short time. Replacement speedos for most models can be found although the cheap ones may be poorly made and inaccurate to the point of illegality in use, and may also require an alternative cable to couple them up. PX EFL models are more of a problem – currently there are only Indian-made versions on sale, but they are not a direct copy. A similar problem exists with MkI T5 units, so check carefully before purchasing as some are described inaccurately.

If you have a rare variant or are particularly attached to the original speedometer, then professional

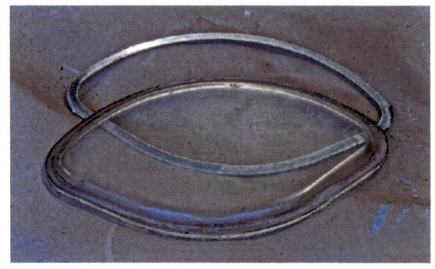

07.43 Speedo glass is held by a crimped chromed ring. It can be levered off from the rear of the speedo head.

restoration can always be arranged at a price.

TRIM

07.44 The plastic faces are often sun damaged, and there is little that can be done to rescue the situation.

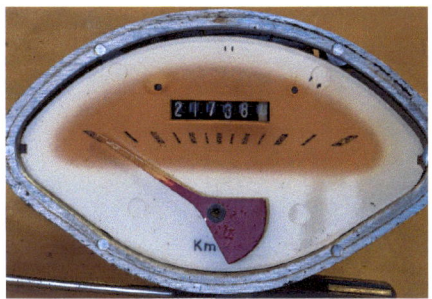

07.45 Speedo needles usually pull off, but may be riveted as in this case. The mechanism itself may be repairable, but the cost will be far more than sourcing a replacement unit.

07.46 PX EFL 'glass' (actually plastic) discolours easily. It is held in place by an outer ring, which is either black or chromed. The easiest way to remove it is to use side cutting pliers, carefully unpeeling the ring once it is split. There is a rubber seal underneath, which needs to be removed and re-used or replaced.

07.47 The new glass and trim push into place and should be secured by rolling the rear edge of the ring around the speedo body. This is a tricky process.

07.48 An alternative is to use Sikkaflex around the ring which also enhances weather sealing. A cable tie will keep it all in place until the sealant has gone off.

STANDS

Replacement chrome stands need inspection before purchase, as there are some very thinly coated ones on sale that corrode almost immediately. Stand fittings can be sourced with ease, but the quality varies.

07.50 Early stand feet are rubber and fit reasonably easily, although warming first in a bucket of hot water can be helpful in cold weather.

07.49 Centre stands and their fittings rust and wear as they are in an exposed position. New parts are available for all models.

HOW TO RESTORE CLASSIC LARGEFRAME VESPA SCOOTERS

07.51 PX-type feet are harder plastic, but a warming from a hot air gun will soften them enough to get them in place.

HORNCAST
Pre-PX these were metal, and either spotwelded in place or part of the legshield pressing. PX versions are plastic, and can be removed by undoing a large self-tapping screw under the top Piaggio badge, and two smaller ones accessed from inside the toolbox. There are several versions depending on model.

07.52 Stand brackets are simply bent pieces of steel, so lubricate the area where the stand sits with grease and treat re-lubrication as part of a regular service schedule. Scooters with 8in wheels (VBB type, not the later Super) will have a single mounting bolt rather than the two shown here. Stand fixing kits with stainless steel bolts can be purchased to replace rusty fittings.

07.53 PX horncasts crack easily as the plastic becomes brittle with age.

07.54 Replacements are cheap but need painting before fitting.

07.55 The top securing screw is hidden under the Piaggio badge. There are two more inside the toolbox.

LEGSHIELD TRIM
A variety of trim is available, although for older models it tends to be multifunctional and may not be a perfect match for the factory fitting, so if originality is paramount then a long search may lie ahead for old stock parts. Most models up to the PX relied on a coated alloy beading which is hand crimped to the legshield. This trim should be fitted

TRIM

to the frame before the headset goes back on.

PXs used a plasticised trim which looks similar to the older alloy version but doesn't need an installation tool. The drawback of the later type is that it is brittle and tricky to fit; a second pair of hands may be needed to hold the trim as it is fed in place. It is an awkward and frustrating job and although many recommend a gentle application of heat to make it easier, it is all too easy to end up discolouring or kinking the new trim. A non-standard alternative is a two-piece solid trim by makers such as Cuppini which is attractive and simple to attach, although all should be treated to some rust inhibitor inside before fitting if the scooter is to be used regularly in the wet.

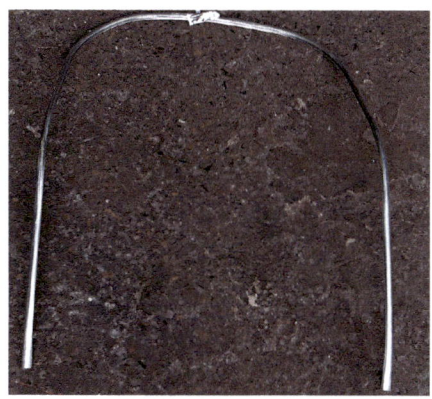

07.56 For most pre-PX scooters the legshield trim is a one-piece alloy pressing. It should be slipped over the legshields and held against them with some tape or even a strap right across. Regardless of method, the new paint must be well dried and protected.

07.57 A special tool is needed to fit it. It is not cheap, so unless it is going to be used on more than one restoration this might be one job where it is easier to hand it over to a local scooter shop.

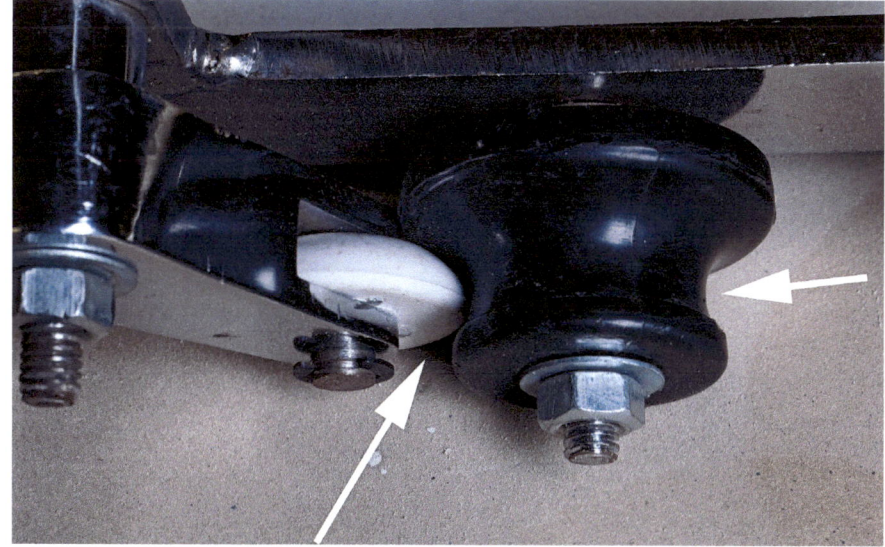

07.58 The trim is trapped between these two rollers (arrowed). The right-hand one sits on the outside of the legshields, the left-hand one presses the trim down into place. The tool should be used from the top working down the legshields. It is difficult to get a good uniform finish in one go, so a couple of runs may be needed.

07.59 Two-piece legshield trim is a popular alternative. It is easy to fit. as it is simply held in place by screws (arrowed). The chrome on even the better stuff can leave a lot to be desired though, so buy a large tin of polish if you want to keep it looking shiny. Stainless steel versions are available, which may be an attractive option.

HOW TO RESTORE CLASSIC LARGEFRAME VESPA SCOOTERS

RUBBER PARTS

Virtually every rubber seal or grommet can be purchased individually or as part of a restoration kit. Toolbox trim comes ready-shaped if it is a genuine part; copies tend to come as one long uniform strip that needs to have the inner edge cut to allow it to bend around the corners. A small amount of adhesive and temporary use of tape may be needed to persuade it to stay in place.

07.60 Rubber kits can be bought if a full restoration is being carried out. They can be a lot cheaper than buying the bits individually.

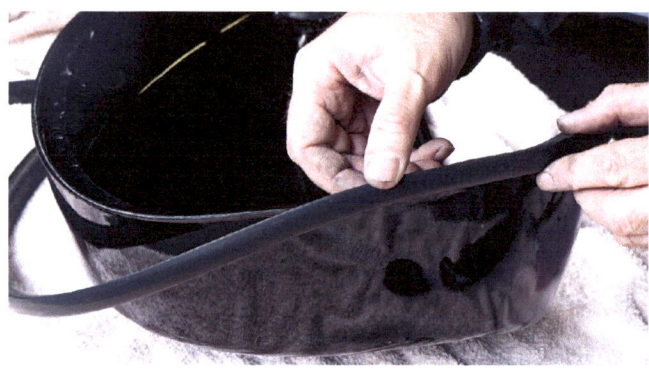

07.61 Side panel trim just pushes into place on all models. Non-genuine stuff may need trimming around the front mounting pin, depending on model.

07.62 PX trim is held at one end by a rivet. If the old trim is being re-used it may be split at this point, so a small washer may be needed under the rivet head to secure it properly.

07.63 Brake and kickstart rubbers just push into place. Cheap versions may be a loose fit and require some adhesive to get them to stay where they're meant to.

TOOLBOX LOCKS

The tool box lids fitted to fixed left-hand side panels are of a similar design to legshield versions, and replacement lock assemblies can be bought for all models.

07.64 Most toolbox locks are held by a sliding plate (bottom arrow) on the rear of the mechanism. PX types are spring-loaded – the spring (top arrow) just pulls free once the locking plate has been pulled away and lock removal started.

TRIM

07.65 The lock's key barrel is held by this spring-loaded tag. Depress the tag and pull the barrel free, using the key to drag it out of the lock.

07.66 Some early models had rivets securing the lock assembly, or even nuts and bolts with some Motovespas. These ones will need to be cut down before the scooter goes back into use.

SPARE WHEEL COVERS

On models that carry a spare wheel under the left-hand side panel, the bottom of the tyre is often covered by a vaguely semicircular panel held in place by a long threaded rod through the rim. Some original '60s style metal covers are now very rare but plastic alternatives are freely available.

HELMET LOCKS

Many models have a bag carrier/helmet holding ring under the nose of the seat. Some aftermarket versions are locking. The assembly is held by two machine screws through the frame, often with a support plate on the inside. PX models have a twin helmet holding plate, which is bolted through the seat hinge with the bolt heads covered when the seat is down.

Chapter 8
Wheels

RIMS

All the rotary valve models use split rims, whether 8in or 10in. The later type are shown in the tyre replacement pictures – the early VBB era rims had a solid centre with a non-symettrical split, but the principles are the same. New rims can be bought for all models. Genuine parts are the best. If your wheels can be re-used after blasting and painting, then that may be the best option. Some cheaper rims distort under the pressure from the inner tube when off the scooter.

TYRE REPLACEMENT

Tyres can be bought with a classic tread to suit period restorations, or with a sportier cut that increases grip. Price is a good indicator of quality with tyres and inner tubes – if you want to save money, it is probably best not to do it here. A variety of liquid puncture prevention products can be bought, which are inserted into the inner tube and can seal minor holes before the tyre deflates. Even if these only manage to slow the process so that the scooter can be safely brought to a halt, they are worth considering.

Tubeless tyres and rims are now available from a few suppliers. Feedback has been varied, so some research may be a good idea. Having said that, updated versions are appearing that seem to have addressed some of the issues.

If you have the ability to carry a spare tyre keep it inflated to the recommended rear tyre pressure – air can always be let out for use on the front if needed. An engine prop stand is also a good idea when out on the road.

08.1 Tyre replacement starts by partially deflating the tube then undoing the rim nuts, which are usually 13mm but on some models may be 14mm.

08.2 The residual air may push open the rim halves slightly, which helps.

08.3 Try pulling away the smaller side of the rim. The chances are it will be stuck on the tyre. Vigorous pulling may get it off – if not, try a pry bar around the edge to get it moving. If the tyre is scrap you can afford to be more aggressive with the bar.

WHEELS

08.4 If it still refuses to budge, stand on the tyre, placing your weight as close to the inner edge as possible, and wiggle from side to side.

08.5 Once one half is off, the inner tube can be removed and the other side of the rim pushed free.

08.6 Clean the rims carefully, removing any old bits of stuck rubber. If they are rusty – which is likely – rub down and treat the corrosion before re-using them. Alternatively have them blasted and repaint inside and out.

08.7 Put the new tyre on the rim half with the valve hole in it. It may take some pushing to drop down enough. If it's tight, lubricate the edge of the tyre with some wet hand soap. Thread the inner tube into the tyre and push the valve through the hole. A sprinkling of talcum powder on the tube will help prevent it sticking to the tyre as you go.

08.8 Inflate the inner just enough to give it some shape, which will help to keep it in place and so prevent the possibility of it being pinched when the other half of the rim is fitted. Make sure that the valve is fully through – you should clearly see the rubber surrounding its base. You may need to support the valve underneath until some air has gone in to hold it in place.

08.9 Push the other rim half down and screw in the first nut and washer. Do not tighten it yet – instead work around the rim adding each nut in turn, then tighten them. Once they are all tight, over-inflate the inner tube slightly and the tyre should pop into the rim edge. Adjust to the required pressure, which completes the job.

STUD REPLACEMENT

Damaged or rusty studs are very common on older scooters. Replacements are cheap, although getting the old ones out can be time-consuming and awkward. Replacement drums can be bought for all the rotary valve models, should stud removal prove impossible.

HOW TO RESTORE CLASSIC LARGEFRAME VESPA SCOOTERS

08.10 Studs rot as shown here, or sometimes the thread gets damaged.

08.11 The back of the stud will have been mushroomed over or staked to prevent it undoing.

08.12 Select a drill bit that sits inside the head of the stud, and drill it out.

08.13 Grab the stud with self-locking grips and unscrew it from the hub. Locking two nuts together risks shearing the stud, but could be tried first. The pliers will destroy the old external threads (white arrow) but the internal ones (red arrow) should be fine. A little heat applied to the area around the stud will help with removal.

08.14 Lock two nuts on the new stud and wind it into the hub. Some locking compound is a good idea too.

08.15 The rear can be mushroomed over, or a chisel used to stake it in a couple of places to lock it in the ear. In either case, fully support the ear of the hub that holds the stud or it will break off.

Chapter 9
Maintenance

Having lavished more time and money on restoring your Vespa than you probably intended, it would be foolish not to keep it in perfect condition and that means regular maintenance. The following schedule should ensure that the scooter provides reliable service.

WEEKLY CHECK
Tyre condition and pressure
Oil tank level (autolube)
Lights and other electrics
Operation of all control cables
Brake fluid level (disc models)

EVERY 1500 MILES/2500KM
Top up gearbox oil
Check sparkplug condition and gap
Adjust cables where required (gearchange, throttle and clutch)
Adjust brake (cables)
Check electrolyte level in battery

EVERY 3000 MILES/5000KM
Check points gap and timing
Adjust idle speed
Change gearbox oil
Clean and check air filter
Lubricate stand pivots
Lubricate lever pivots
Check wheel nuts and other fittings for security

EVERY 6000 MILES/10,000KM
Change sparkplug
Replace points and condenser
Remove drums, check linings front and rear, lubricate brake cam pivots
Grease front wheel bearings
Grease gear selector box
Lubricate all cables (not nylon lined)

EVERY 12000 MILES/20,000KM
Replace brake fluid (this should be done bi-annually regardless of mileage)

EVERY 24000/40,000KM
De-coke cylinder head and piston
Check rings for wear
De-coke exhaust system

FUEL AND OIL
Your Vespa was originally designed to run on low-grade fuel and is perfectly happy with standard unleaded (95 RON). Always use a good quality semi-synthetic two-stroke oil as they provide a good balance between cost and enhanced engine protection. A move to fully synthetic will certainly do no harm other than to your wallet. It is often suggested that choosing one oil manufacturer and sticking to it is preferable to chopping and changing, although there does not appear to be any hard and fast evidence to back that position. Having said that, many owners will have their own preferred brand and stick to it. Always turn off the petrol tap on pre-mix models before adding the two-stroke oil. Although a de-coke is listed at 24,000 miles it probably will not be necessary thanks to modern low ash oils, so unless performance has dropped, which may suggest a degree of gumming or even piston ring wear, it may not be worth the effort.

Vespa gearbox oil has a hard life, so change it within 500 miles/800km on a newly rebuilt engine, then revert to the foregoing schedule (although changing it every 1500 miles/3000km would do no harm). If it comes out

HOW TO RESTORE CLASSIC LARGEFRAME VESPA SCOOTERS

very black and smells burnt, the clutch plates are wearing out. If a magnetic drain plug is fitted, expect to find fine swarf at each change, but there should be no large chunks.

CABLES

Cable maintenance is greatly reduced if you have chosen to fit nylon-lined versions, as they require no lubrication and give a smoother feel to the controls as well. If you're running the older cable, consider investing in a dedicated oiler – it will make life a lot easier. Remember to lightly grease the lever and other pivot points as well.

STORAGE

If you are going to lay up your scooter over the winter, or any other time for that matter, there are a few sensible precautions to take. First, run the engine with the fuel tap turned off until the motor dies, which will empty the carb of petrol – if left it will separate and leave a sticky mess in the float bowl. Opinions vary on whether to leave the tank full or empty. If full, there is less risk of internal rusting, but the whole lot may need draining if left for too long as the petrol goes off, and in a pre-mix scooter the oil may separate. Consider starting the engine and running it once a month, then running the carb dry again to help keep

09.1 Fully synthetic may be a needless expense for Vespas in standard tune. This stuff from SIP in Germany, however, is as cheap as other brands' semi synthetic oils.

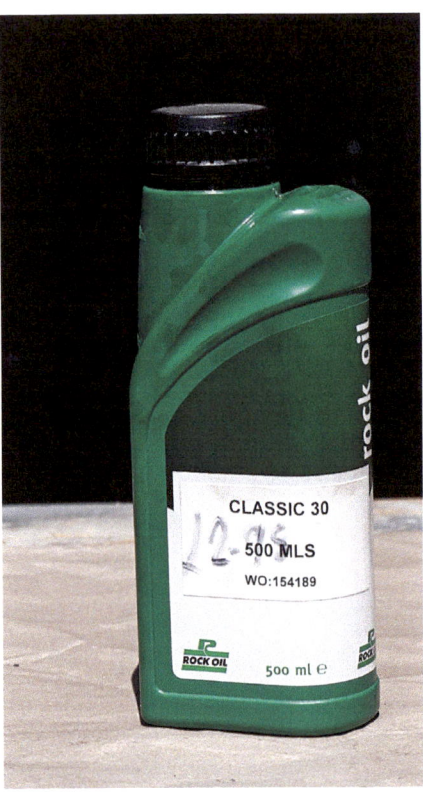

09.2 Most users seem to prefer a classic straight 30 formulation in the gearbox.

everything flowing as it should. The gearbox should not be left with old oil in it, as bearing surfaces can be attacked by contaminants; change it before laying up the scooter. Keep the battery (where fitted) topped up with a dedicated storage trickle charger, or take it off and do it once a month with a normal charger. Make sure the scooter is clean and polished, then prop both wheels off the ground to take the pressure off the tyres. A breathable cover is essential if the scooter is left outside. If stored inside, simply covering with a light cotton sheet should be enough.

ALSO FROM VELOCE –

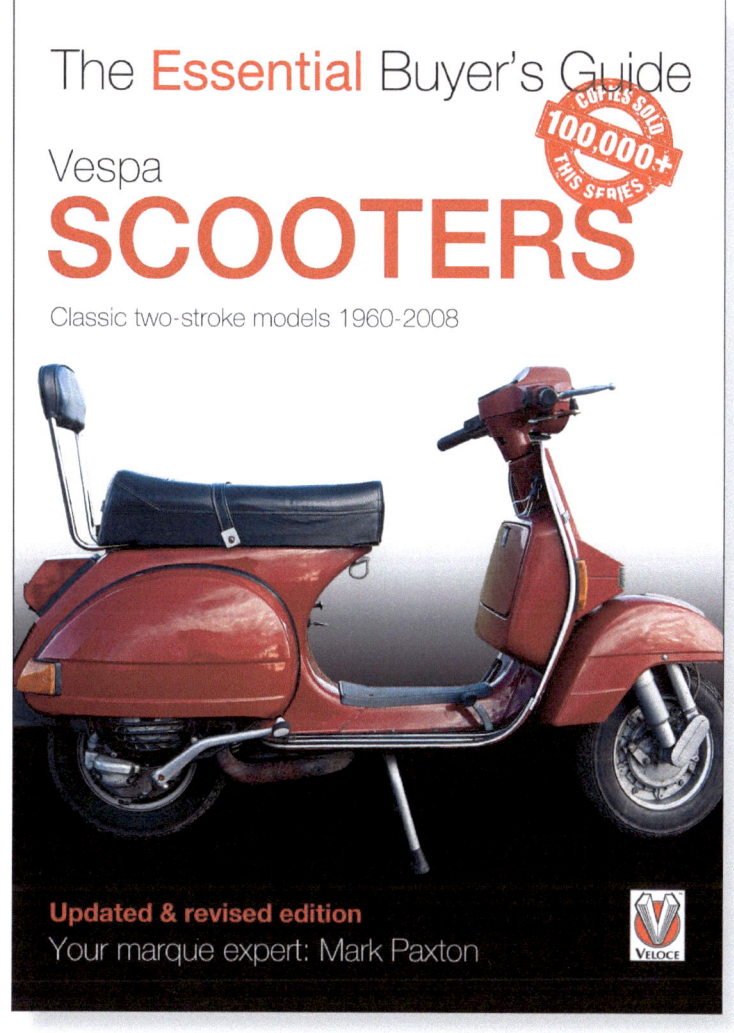

ISBN: 978-1-845848-83-5
Paperback • 19.5x13.9cm • £12.99* UK/$19.95* USA • 64 pages
• 99 colour pictures

Stop! Don't buy a classic Vespa without buying this book first! Having this book in your pocket is just like having a real marque expert by your side. Learn how to spot a bad scooter quickly and how to assess a promising one like a professional. Get the right classic Vespa at the right price!

For more info on Veloce titles, visit our website at www.veloce.co.uk • email: info@veloce.co.uk
• Tel: +44(0)1305 260068
* prices subject to change, p&p extra

ALSO FROM VELOCE –

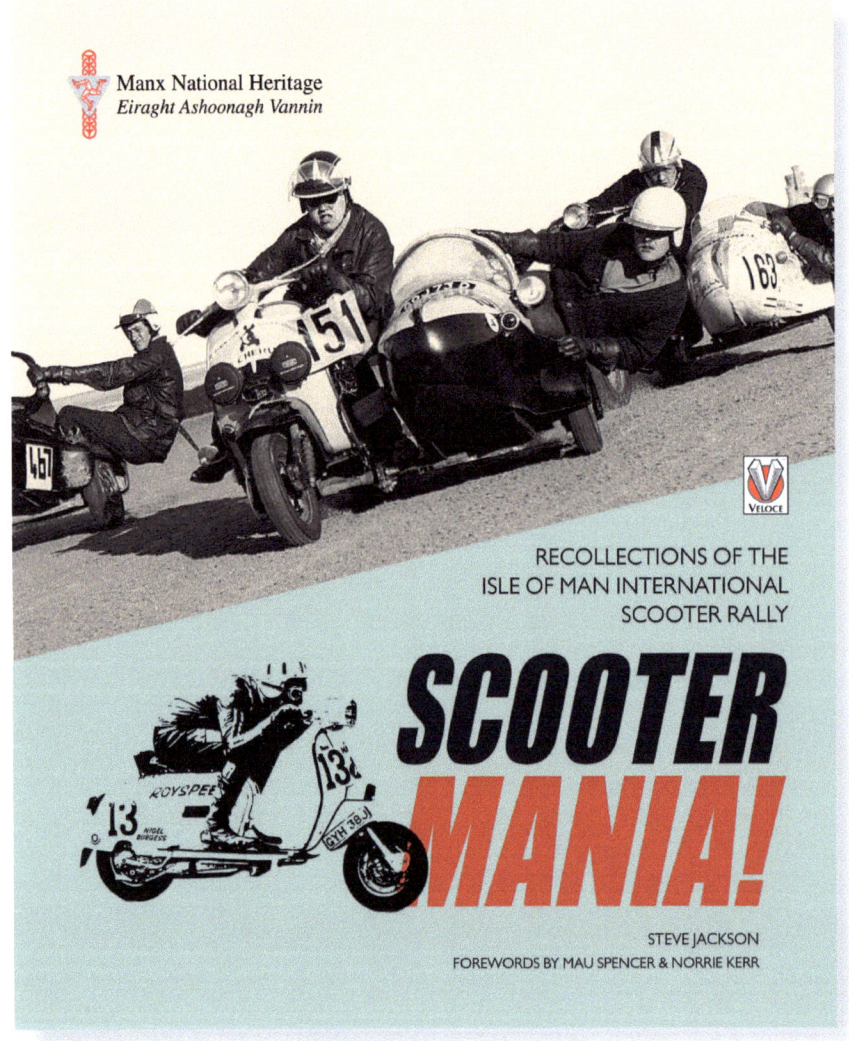

ISBN: 978-1-845846-48-0
Paperback • 25x20.7cm • £14.99* UK/$25* USA • 128 pages
• 180 colour and b&w pictures

At last! A year-on-year account of the Isle of Man International Scooter Rally, including competitors' and organisers' personal experiences, and the controversies and difficulties experienced by the Rally Committee in what became a remarkable, 20-year chapter in the history of scootering sport. Events included endurance and navigational trials, hillclimbs, scrambling, gymkhana competitions, circuit and closed road racing, assembly rallies and sand racing. Supported by 180 images from the period.

For more info on Veloce titles, visit our website at www.veloce.co.uk • email: info@veloce.co.uk
• Tel: +44(0)1305 260068
* prices subject to change, p&p extra

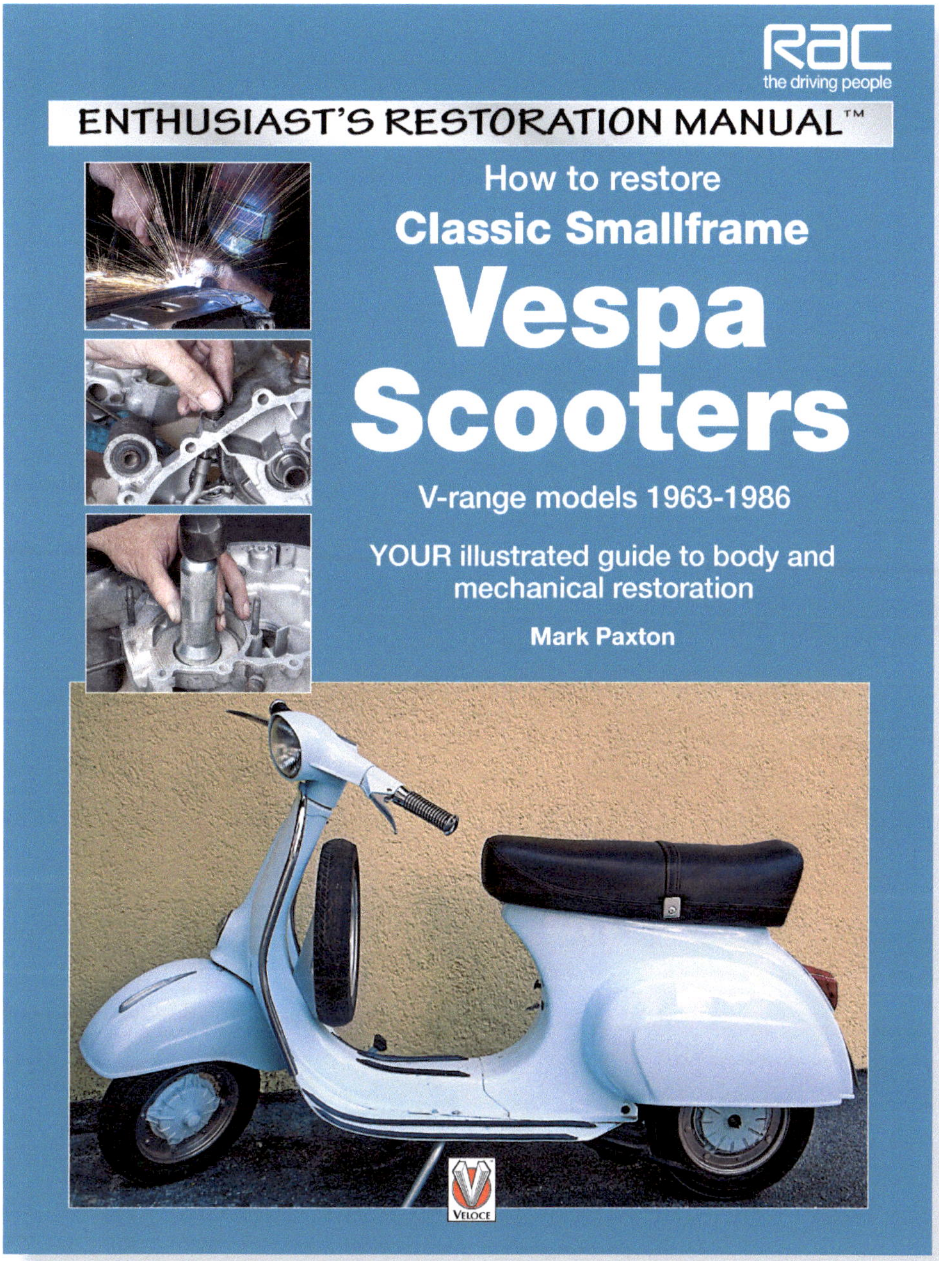

How to restore Classic Smallframe Vespa Scooters

ENTHUSIAST'S RESTORATION MANUAL™

V-range models 1963-1986

YOUR illustrated guide to body and mechanical restoration

Mark Paxton

ISBN: 978-1-845844-37-0
Paperback • 27x20.7cm • £19.99* UK/$39.95* USA • 120 pages
• over 650 colour and b&w pictures

This book investigates the reality of smallframe Vespa restoration in detail. Aimed at the do-it-yourself enthusiast and featuring over 600 clear colour photographs, it is an essential step-by step-guide to the complete renovation of your beloved scooter.

For more info on Veloce titles, visit our website at www.veloce.co.uk • email: info@veloce.co.uk
• Tel: +44(0)1305 260068
* prices subject to change, p&p extra

ALSO FROM VELOCE –

ISBN: 978-1-845840-95-2
Paperback • 21x14.8cm • £9.99* UK/$19.95* USA • 80 pages
• 89 colour pictures

Aimed at the rider who wants to do his or her own basic scooter maintenance and servicing without the need for in-depth mechanical knowledge, or a technical manual. A must-have for scooter users.

For more info on Veloce titles, visit our website at www.veloce.co.uk • email: info@veloce.co.uk
• Tel: +44(0)1305 260068
* prices subject to change, p&p extra

Index

Badges 138, 139
Barrel 15, 50
Bearings crankshaft 27, 28, 30-32
Bearings hub 83-86, 93-95
Bearings pivot 84, 85, 96, 97
Bearings steering head 102-105
Brake caliper 99-102
Brake master cylinder 75-78
Brake pedal 118, 119
Brake shoes front 80, 87, 88
Brake shoes rear 21, 22, 47, 48

Cables 12, 90, 119, 120, 154
Carburettor 11, 23, 48, 61-64
Charging system 137
Chassis number 8
Choke assembly 11, 62
Clutch overhaul 41-46
Clutch removal 19, 20
Coil 136
Crankshaft 25, 26, 33
Cruciform 38-38
Cush drive 33-36
Cylinder 15, 50
Cylinder head 14, 51

Decarbonisation 14
Dent removal 115, 116

Engine mounts 52-54
Engine number 8
Engine removal 10-13
Exhaust system 12, 65

Filler 124, 125
Flywheel 17, 49
Floor box sections 112-114
Floor replacement 108-111
Floor runners 140, 141
Fork bearings 83-85, 96, 97
Fork overhaul: early 78-90
Fork overhaul: late 91-99
Frame number 8
Fuel tank 57, 58
Fuel tap 59, 60

Gasket, barrel 50
Gasket, case 41
Gearbox 26, 27, 36-39

Headlight 66, 131
Headset: early 66-72
Headset: PX 72-75
Horncast 146

Ignition, electronic 136
Ignition points 133, 134

Ignition timing 134, 135
Indicators 131, 132
Inner tubes 150, 151

Jets (carburettor) 61

Kickstart assembly 27, 40

Legshield trim 147
Levers 67, 75
Little end (con rod) 16, 50
Lock, steering 120-122

Maintenance 153, 154
Mudguard 79, 90, 118

Oil 154
Oil tank 58, 59

Paint 123, 127
Paint removal 106, 107
Panel trim 139, 148
Panels 117, 118
Piston and rings 16, 50, 51
Primer 126, 127

Sealer 127
Seat 142-144

HOW TO RESTORE CLASSIC LARGEFRAME VESPA SCOOTERS

Seat cover 143, 144
Selector box 51, 52
Sparkplug 136
Speedo 67, 71-73, 144, 145
Spring, front 89, 92
Stand 145, 146

Stator plate 18, 133
Studs, cylinder 15, 49, 50
Studs, wheel 152

Timing disc 135
Toolbox 118, 148, 149

Tyres 150, 151

Wheels 150
Wiring 129, 130

Xmas tree 26